Dear Diane

LETTERS FROM
THE FIRST GULF WAR

DEAR DIANE

Letters From
the First Gulf War

Printed in the United States of America

First Printing: July 2010

Night Flight Press, LLC
P.O. Box 2634
Decatur, GA 30031

ISBN 978-1-4507-1277-4

FOR
Those who wait, wonder, worry and pray
for loved ones in harm's way.

Contents

Appendices

A. Reflections of a Soldier in the Gulf

B. Reflections on the Vietnam War Memorial

C. Farewell Address to the 1st Battalion 69th Armor

Introduction

This book grew from one of my least favorite chores: cleaning the basement. As I was moving boxes and sorting old papers around the spring of 2008, I made a discovery that stopped me in my tracks. In one non-descript box, I found the letters that I had written to my wife, Diane, while I was deployed during Operation Desert Shield/ Desert Storm from August 1990 through February 1991. Unbeknownst to me, Diane had saved every one of them.

Many years had passed since I had even given that period of my life any sustained thought. But when I found those letters, it was a powerful jolt back to my deployment as part of a tank battalion in the Army. In some ways, it was a very good time of my life. In other ways, however, it was the most difficult. So I was understandably hesitant about reliving the memories. For several days after finding the letters, I didn't do anything with them. I just left them there.

Then, a few days later, I started the process of organizing the letters by date. I didn't read them, though – I wasn't ready for the emotion of that yet. I simply sorted them by the date at the top of each letter, putting them in crisp manila folders, one for each month. And then I set them aside again.

Finally, I made the decision to go back in time almost 20 years. It was almost surreal to think that two decades had passed since that time. It was the days before the prevalence of e-mail, text messages, and social networking. The main means of communication back then – at least, cross-continental communication – was letters. And here were dozens of mine, in my own handwriting, on pages and pages of notebook paper and legal pads.

And as I read my own words in my own hand, I snapped right back into my mindset back then: a stranger in a strange land, wondering when, or if, I would return to my wife one day. At this point, I don't feel the need to summarize the array of emotions I experienced in the deserts of Saudi Arabia and Iraq; in this respect, the letters speak for themselves.

They're organized in chronological order, from month to month. In most of the letters, I included the time – in military time, of course – at the top right-hand corner along with the date. I have no idea why I was so anal about recording the times, but I was. I guess it was because sometimes, I wrote to Diane more than once a day, and I somehow thought that the time of day I was writing was relevant.

It's also important to note my process in presenting the letters. My first step was to type them all up from their original handwritten format. The only editing used was minor corrections in grammar (and cleaning up of some of the typos that resulted from transcribing the letters), and the philosophy behind that was to make them easier to read. Some references to proper nouns, like titles of books or magazines, are purposely not italicized in order to preserve the way the letters were originally written. In addition, in a few instances, I decided to remove or shorten the name or names of fellow soldiers. I wanted to be truthful without being hurtful. Except for those minor changes, what follows in this book is exactly what I wrote.

What I hope comes through the strongest in my letters is this: how lucky I was to have a wonderful wife to write to at home. I was able to stay (relatively) sane for the simple fact that I knew Diane was there for me. I owe her a tremendous debt of gratitude for saving the letters, for preserving my history and our shared history, and for keeping the memories alive. My purpose in publishing these letters is to acknowledge and honor my wife's love and support publicly. And, just as importantly, I'd like to recognize how important that kind of love and support is to all who serve in foreign lands. This book went to press as the 20th anniversary of the start of the first Persian Gulf War, also known as Desert Shield/Desert Storm, approached, and it was a fitting time for this sort of a tribute.

INTRODUCTION

Family separation, like the kind that's all too often caused by overseas military deployments, is so difficult. The strain that it puts on everything – from personal relationships to family finances – can be unbearable. Sometimes, sadly, the relationships just don't survive.

In many ways, however, the separation can be easier for the soldier who is deployed. Certainly, being deployed in a war zone is rife with danger. But that kind of potential peril tends to focus the mind. Survival is the objective and it does not leave much room for wistful thinking. A certain mission-centric mentality sets in, one in which training takes over. You're trained to follow orders, do what you're told to do, and there's not much room for interpretation.

At the same time, you don't know which bullet has your name on it, and in that atmosphere of uncertainty, a kind of clarity permeates. The soldier understands his place in the world. He knows what his mission is, whether it is narrow or broad. And in a strange way, this kind of simplicity offers a great deal of comfort.

But what about those who remain behind: the spouses, children, mothers, fathers, siblings of the deployed soldiers? Their knowledge of their loved one's status is limited, which causes another level of distress that I feel is woefully underappreciated. What's worse than knowing bad news is not knowing anything at all. And for the loved ones waiting and wondering, this is very often the case. While I was deployed, I think Diane became closer to CNN's Wolf Blitzer than to almost anyone else, because he could provide the best possible information about our deployment.

I know that support systems exist for military families. In fact, the military actually does a good job with this. But what I see lacking is a collective support by our nation of those families. Since the percentage of military families is so small compared to the population of our country – 1.4 million active duty personnel and more than 850,000 National Guard or other military reserves for a nation of 300-plus million – I suppose that's to be expected. But it should not be accepted.

As I write these words, the United States is engaged in wars in both Iraq and Afghanistan. American soldiers are deployed in various other places around the world. But I'd like to clarify something I think is a major misconception: The United States is not a *country* at war; we are a country whose *military branches* are at war. When we flip on the evening news or open the newspaper and hear or see how many lives are lost that day or week, it's all too often just a number to the majority of the population.

But for the military wife, or husband, or mother or father or sibling of a soldier, those figures mean so much more. It's so easy for most of us to stop and pause when we hear the death count, and maybe feel sad for a minute or two, and then move on to something else. But it's a much darker, potentially devastating story for anyone with a loved one in the war zone. Imagine hearing the latest casualty count and wondering, "Is my husband (or wife) among them?" Or having to explain to a four-year-old over and over that Mommy or Daddy will be home soon. Or hearing that your spouse's deployment has been extended – yet again. All of this on top of the fact that most military spouses are holding down a household and raising children by themselves during deployments.

Such sacrifices and hardships need to be recognized, appreciated and honored so much more in the collective mindset than they currently are. Publishing this book has been a strong reminder that I need to do a better job of this on a personal level as well.

I also want to say a word about the lost art of letter writing. As someone who loves words and the English language, I lament what interpersonal communication has become today. Technology is a wonderful thing, and I embrace it. But all this e-mailing and texting and Twittering has come with a cost. While we send immediate, witty responses to every insignificant snippet that comes across the transom, we seem to have forgotten how to express thoughtful reflection. We send clipped messages to friends, peppered with OMGs and LOLs, neglecting proper sentence structure and thoughtful word choices. I know I sound like some know-it-all fuddy-duddy English teacher lamenting today's youth and their newfangled gadgetry, but I'm okay with that; I still believe that our beautiful language is being butchered by technology.

Furthermore, I believe that too many people growing up today have never experienced a simple joy in life: receiving a letter. Think about it: When was the last time you received a handwritten letter from someone? How did it make you feel? And when is the last time that you wrote one? The sound of pen to paper is a beautiful thing. I'm talking about a page or more of words, not just scratching out a shopping list.

If the physical act of writing a letter isn't motivation enough, then try this: Think of someone you care deeply about. Think about what they mean to you. Think about how important your relationship with them is to you. And then sit down and write that person a letter. In your own hand, in your own words – just write. The written word can be a very powerful thing – it's like free therapy! And you might be very surprised at how profound an impact that simple act has on the recipient of your letter – and on you. I highly encourage you to try it.

As I re-read my letters for the first time, I was amazed by how prolific I was. I wrote to Diane almost every day – sometimes for pages and pages – and for that I am very proud. And I'm just grateful that I had a loved one to whom I could write. Writing those letters helped me survive a tremendously difficult time in my life. I treasure them, and they will be in my possession until the day I leave this world.

But as you're about to see for yourself, the letters themselves are not masterpieces in any way. There are times when my sentence structure is poor, my word choice is weak and there's not much exciting subject matter. On a personal level, they are simply the musings of a lonely and sometimes frightened husband who missed his wife. On a larger scale, however, they are reflective of something much more profound: the struggle and sacrifice that thousands of military families deal with every day.

one

AUGUST 1990

Separation

O n August 2, 1990, a man whom I had never heard of – Saddam Hussein – invaded a country that I had never heard of – Kuwait – and set in motion the chain of events that led to my eventual deployment to the Middle East, and the subsequent letters that I wrote to my wife while I was there.

I entered active military service when I signed in for the Armor Officer's Basic Course (AOBC) at Ft. Knox, Kentucky, on May 19, 1986. The United States was in the midst of The Cold War, which was the continuing state of tension that existed between the Soviet Union and its satellites and the powers of the Western World, led by the United States. Little did any of us know at the time that we had already entered the last phase of The Cold War, because our training focus was Soviet centric: their weapons, tactics and capabilities.

Of course, we now know that The Cold War ended without the two superpowers ever fighting each other directly. In November 1989, the Berlin Wall came down, and the Soviet Union as such no longer exists. But in 1986, all of us freshly minted second lieutenants were convinced that we would eventually have to duke it out with those guys in the mother of all land combat, and the battle would most likely be fought in Europe. As we trained, this thought was always in the back of our minds. Little did we know that the war we would actually fight would be in a very different place against a very different foe.

But before I go any more into that challenge awaiting us in the desert, some necessary back story: that of Diane and me.

DEAR DIANE

Diane and I met in the summer of 1984. At the time, I was a student at Armstrong State College in Savannah, Georgia, and was working nights as a doorman at the Night Flight Café, one of the city's best live music venues. It had jazz, blues, fusion, you name it – I saw the B-52's and 10,000 Maniacs there before they hit big. Diane came in with a friend of mine, Sandy, whom I'd known for several years. I let them both in for free, which I guess she thought was a nice gesture.

Later in the evening, Diane had asked the bartender, a buddy of mine, what I liked to drink, and she bought me a Scotch for letting her in free. There weren't any sparks, though. I made a nice gesture, she made a nice gesture, and that was kind of the end of it.

Or so I thought.

Later that evening our paths crossed again at another of Savannah's popular watering holes, Pinkie Masters. I was there with the girl I was dating at time. As usual, my girlfriend wound up hanging out with her own friends, and I found myself sitting in a booth across from Diane, whom I'd met a few hours earlier. We just sat and talked, without any ulterior motives. During our chat I found out she'd recently relocated to Savannah from Madison, Wisconsin, where she'd lived for about eight years.

She struck me as immediately different from some of the other women I'd met in Savannah – she didn't pepper her speech with any of the typical Southern niceties I'd gotten so used to. For example, I used to wear Izod, which was the hot style of the day, and at one point in the conversation she looked me in the eye and said, "So, is that alligator supposed to make you look cool or what?" It caught me off guard – and totally sparked my interest.

After a while, I left with my girlfriend. The girlfriend didn't last, but the impression Diane had made in that booth did.

In the weeks that followed, Diane and I kept running into each other, until I finally asked her if she wanted to run into each other on purpose. Our first official date was at Pinkie Masters, the spot where we'd originally connected. For the first year that we went out, though, she had no idea about my military involvement and my impending call to active duty. I didn't really think it was necessary to bring it up, for several reasons. First of all, I had no idea about our future, and second, though I wouldn't describe Diane at the time as anti-military, she wasn't pro-military either. But as my military obligations came into a sharper focus, and that active-duty commitment date loomed closer, I knew I couldn't keep it a secret any longer.

Diane was initially surprised and disappointed, but because the date wasn't immediate, it didn't affect us. However, it eventually began to. I finished my degree requirements in March 1986, and instead of hanging around to attend my graduation ceremony in June, I opted to get going with my active duty service in May. I just wanted to get on with my life after school.

So, upon my departure to Kentucky, for my AOBC training, Diane and I decided that we'd make a go of things between us. She came to visit me in Kentucky, and we met in Atlanta several times, and for a while our relationship was great. We were able to stay close and see each other fairly often. But, toward the end of my training in Kentucky, I got my permanent assignment orders to go to Germany. And that's when we faced a critical decision: stay together or split up.

I knew I loved her, and I knew I wanted to marry her, but I was a little concerned that I was too young for such a critical life step: I was only 23, while she was 31. I remember going to dinner one night, and Diane just told me, straight up, that she loved me, and she wanted to be with me, but if I thought I would just go to Germany, complete my tour and come back three years later to find her waiting for me, I was – to put it politely – absolutely nuts.

I took that to heart, but left for Kitzingen, West Germany, a few days later without a resolution to what we would do.

Once I arrived in Germany, I was pleased to discover I really liked it – it was a beautiful country with nice people and great beer, and I had a challenging, fulfilling job. But I realized very quickly that I missed Diane more than I thought I would – and that I wanted her in my life. So I asked her if she would come visit, and she came in January 1987 for two weeks. At that point, I asked her to marry me – with the caveat that she had to pull our wedding together in three months, because I had a brief window in April from maneuver exercises.

Diane pulled everything off beautifully – and we had not just one, but three, wedding receptions, thrown by various family and friends, in Savannah and in Madison and Bonduel, Wisconsin, her hometown. The first, and the official, ceremony was in Savannah on April 11, 1987, a beautiful spring day and the day after my birthday. It was the best present I could have ever asked for.

From there, we spent several days in Hilton Head, South Carolina, relaxing and recouping. Diane had laryngitis, but once she was feeling better we made the trek north, stopping to see friends along the way. We had an extra case of champagne leftover from the wedding, which we stored in the trunk. Every night we'd pop a bottle and toast our happiness with our friends.

Once we arrived in Madison, longtime friends of Diane, Gus and Mary Paraskevoulakus, threw us a fantastic reception at their Greek restaurant, Kosta's. It was one great party and we still talk about it today. Then Diane's family threw us another reception party in Bonduel, at the American Legion Hall, so I could get to know the relatives I'd not yet met. During the evening, I was "kidnapped" by some of her friends for a bar-hopping tour around town, and they succeeded in getting me severely drunk. Ah, the memories of the newlywed days.

From there, I headed back to West Germany, while Diane prepared to join me in a few months. Our three-year tour in Germany, from 1986 to 1989, was a highlight of my time in the military. Diane found a good job working as a nurse in the Army Hospital, and we used our weekends to travel all around Europe.

In late 1989, we left West Germany and returned to Ft. Knox, Kentucky so I could attend my Armor Officer's Advanced Course (AOAC). The Berlin Wall was now gone, what had been the Soviet Union was crumbling and the political discourse in the United States began to bubble with a strange new lexicon. To this day I wonder whatever happened to the so-called "peace dividend."

I completed AOAC in June 1990. After that, Diane drove to Wisconsin to spend some time with her family before joining me at our next duty station. Meanwhile, I headed south to Ft. Benning, Georgia, where I was to be assigned to the 2nd Battalion, 69th Armor as part of the 197th Infantry Brigade. Later the Brigade became the 3rd Brigade of the 24th Infantry Division. A few weeks after my arrival in southwest Georgia, our world turned upside down with Saddam Hussein's invasion of Kuwait on August 2, 1990. Within days, we were mobilizing for what came to be known as Operation Desert Shield.

Looking back, I cannot say that the initial news of Iraq's invasion of Kuwait set off any particular alarm bells in my mind. I failed to see the full scope of its eventual impact. But shortly thereafter, our Commander-in-Chief, President George H.W. Bush, calmly and resolutely said, "This aggression will not stand." And I knew that was the beginning of something big – for our world as a whole, and for my own.

Diane and I had been apart before – anyone in the military knows it's a life of separations. But what was to happen next was unprecedented in the time that we had been together.

Within days, we were mobilizing for our deployment. Days later, we were en route to Ft. Stewart/Hunter Army Airfield, in Georgia, which was to be our embarkation point. The next stop would be The Kingdom of Saudi Arabia.

I had no idea what we'd be facing in this desert land, this new environment. As a soldier, I didn't really give it too much thought. At the end of the day, I was going to do what I was ordered to do and take whatever came as it came. It was a matter of thinking, I'm gonna get to do what I've been training to do, and I managed to squash other thoughts of trepidation and fear. I sensed some differing emotions among fellow soldiers, though. The youngest ones, the junior enlisted soldiers, seemed the most anxious, as did the oldest soldiers, those who had managed to get through a long military career without having to face combat. The soldiers closer to my age, who had been too young to fight in the Vietnam War but had still been on active duty for 15 or 20 years, were the most calm of anyone.

Still, it was a very uneasy time for everyone – especially spouses. In the back of every soldier's mind, the thought of an actual deployment to a combat zone is always there, and loved ones feel that fear, too. But that gets suppressed as you go about trying to live your normal life and be happy. Now that this possibility had become reality – I could die – Diane and I had to talk about things that we had never before.

As preparations ramped up, Diane and I tried to talk about what she would do if I didn't make it back. But we could never complete those conversations because that potential reality was too difficult to comprehend. It was as if acknowledging it would somehow make it come to pass. So we operated under the assumption that I would deploy, do my duty and come home, whenever that was, unscathed.

The night before I left, we tried to have dinner as usual at our apartment in Columbus, Georgia. But neither of us could eat. We went to bed and lay there, not talking but not sleeping.

Early the next morning, I loaded up my green duffel bag and a rucksack into Diane's red Nissan 240 SX, and she drove me to Battalion Headquarters on Fort Benning. We sat there in the car in the parking lot, immersed in silence and still not really believing that this was real, and hugged each other for a long time. Diane sobbed, but I somehow managed to hold the tears back. I was trying to be strong for her and for myself, trying to get into a mindset that was ready for battle. We told each other that we loved each other, and I got out of the car to unload my gear.

We said our final goodbyes, and I waved and attempted to smile, trying to give Diane the sense that it would all be okay. She never got out of the car, and I watched her drive away. It was the saddest moment of my life, because I honestly didn't know if I would ever see my wife again.

Our battalion of approximately 500 soldiers boarded big, cushy touring buses and made the trip to Fort Stewart, Georgia, where we stayed for a week or two for some additional training. Then, we headed to Hunter Army Airfield in Savannah, which was our last stop before Saudia Arabia.

After saying goodbye to Diane, I thought that was the last time I'd have to go through something that emotionally difficult. But I was wrong. The details are a little fuzzy, but I guess I'd mentioned to my mom beforehand that we'd be making a brief stop in Savannah before deploying to the Middle East. I knew I wouldn't have time to go see her, and I was fine with that – at that time, I was trying to get myself into a war-focused mindset.

As we were loading up our gear, a fellow soldier came up to me and said, "Captain Bradshaw, there's someone at the fence who wants to talk to you." I had no idea who that would be, but to my surprise and delight my mom, Mary, and my sister, Alethia, were on the other side of the chain link fence. Somehow, my mom had found out we were leaving that day and managed to locate me in a sea of hundreds of soldiers all wearing the same uniform.

We talked for a few minutes, and I remember my mom telling me that she loved me and that she would be praying for me. Alethia, who was around 22, didn't say very much. We eventually said our goodbyes, but before I joined my fellow soldiers, I had to find a place by myself, where no one would see me absolutely lose it. I don't remember where I went, but I do remember it wasn't easy finding a spot with some privacy; there were soldiers swarming everywhere. I finally did, though, and just cried and cried for several minutes. Saying goodbye to my mom and my sister through that chain link fence as I headed off to war was one of the most emotional moments of my life.

Saying goodbye to my mom was something I hadn't planned on doing – I had avoided it, in fact. And, at the time, I wasn't sure the visit did me very much good, because it put me back in a very emotional place right before we headed off into a war zone. But with 20 years of hindsight, their coming to see me was a wonderful gesture. It underscored the fact that I was loved and cared for, and there's nothing better than knowing that, especially as you're headed somewhere from which you know you may not return.

AUGUST 1990

Dear Diane,

This is probably the hardest letter I have ever had to write. There is so much that I wish to say to you. There are probably a lot of things I wish I had not said at times. But, the past cannot be changed.

I don't know how events will play out. I am a little unnerved. But, I fully intend to return home to you hopefully unscarred mentally or physically.

I know I have not always been the husband that you want me to be. I know there have been times when I have seemed thoughtless, uncaring and downright mean. But, I want you to know that I have never intentionally hurt you. Nor would I ever want to. You don't deserve it.

Sometimes you have been a gigantic pain in the ass. ☺ But, all-in-all you have been a wonderful wife. You have been all that I've wanted and more. At times you have been better to me than I have been to myself. For that I am eternally grateful.

I know that you love me. And I will carry the knowledge of that love with me into the desert. I trust that it will sustain me through whatever lies ahead. But, if for some reason I'm unable to return to you as you know me now, you have to know this: I love you more now than I did on the day that we married. I love you more than I have ever loved anyone. I love you more than life itself. I love you mucho de mucho. And I will carry that love with me throughout eternity.

Always,
Stephen

two

SEPTEMBER 1990

Deployment

J ust before midnight on August 31, 1990, the 2nd Battalion 69th Armor landed in Ad Damman, Saudi Arabia, a port city on the banks of the Persian Gulf. I – along with the rest of my battalion – was officially a stranger in a strange land.

Descending from the plane, it felt like I had stepped into a sauna. The temperature must have been in the high 90s, with the humidity so thick you could almost grab hold of it. I thought to myself, *If it's this hot here at almost midnight, what in hell must the days be like?* I would soon discover that highs approaching 120 degrees were not uncommon.

My fellow soldiers and I had no clue as to what the next few days, weeks and months would hold for us and, curiosity and bravado aside, we were also very nervous. The pilots and flight attendants who took care of us on every leg of our trip must have sensed that. Flying commercial airliners was significantly better than military transport planes, but they made the trip even better with their treatment of us. Regardless of rank, they made us all feel like silver elite passengers flying first class. I will always be grateful for that.

The 2nd Battalion 69th Armor consisted of more than 550 men and 64 tanks, in addition to various other combat equipment. To the military-minded man, the M1 Abrams main battle tank was indeed a thing of beauty: two tons of steel and state-of-the-art technology. Its fire-control system, the mechanism that guides the actual tank round, had a laser range finder that made for very accurate shooting. It was the most advanced weapon of its type at the time.

But, as we landed in Saudi Arabia and got settled in the tent city that would become home, our tanks and all of our other equipment were still on transport ships. They would arrive, no question, but they were still days away. For that unsettling time, we were actually a tank battalion without any tanks – rendering us virtually useless in terms of war fighting capability. We had our personal weapons, but that was about it.

I never felt more vulnerable. If the Iraqi regime had its eye on invading Saudi Arabia, this would have been the time. Nevertheless, I felt we were ready to deal with whatever headed our way.

Prior to our arrival in Saudi Arabia, I'd been assigned as the Assistant Staff Officer for Operations (Asst. S-3) for the battalion, and eventually became the Staff Officer for Personnel and Administration (S-1). I had previously been the S-1 in Germany, and the battalion commander thought he needed someone with experience in that role. S-1 is a necessary but thankless job. After we first arrived and were still waiting for our equipment, I turned my attention to making sure all of our men were accounted for. At the time, the entire battalion was concentrated in a pretty tight space because the companies – individual units within the battalion – hadn't yet spread out through the desert since our equipment hadn't yet arrived. Every morning and every afternoon, we had roll call for the entire battalion to make sure everyone was accounted for, and I was in charge of that.

In addition, I would run the Administration and Logistics Operations Center (ALOC), a secondary command post that would take over operations in case the Tactical Operations Center, or TOC, was taken out. I performed this job, along with my partner, the battalion S-4, for the duration. It should be noted that none of the staff positions are really that glorious, and these were no exception. But, essentially all new captains have to do their staff time before they can move on to command tank companies, which was my goal. So I accepted my role with clarity, humility and a desire to perform well.

Getting from Ft. Benning to Ft. Stewart to Hunter Army Airfield to Saudi Arabia had been a whirlwind, and the days had passed quickly. Now, in the desert, waiting for our equipment to arrive, time slowed to a crawl. I had plenty of time to sit around and think. As a result the reality of the situation began to set in. I started to miss my wife and my life back in the United States very much.

4 SEPTEMBER, 1990
0755 HRS.

Dear Diane,

I'm sorry that it has taken me so long to write to you. The last several days have been pretty hectic. But, I'm pretty well settled now. Right now we are living in "tent city" right at the port in Ad Damman, Saudi Arabia. We'll be here until our equipment arrives, which should be around 7 or 8 September. Once we get our stuff we'll be moving to positions about 100 km north of here out in the middle of nowhere.

The weather, as expected, has been HOT! Yesterday's high was 112 degrees. They say the place we are going is about 5-10 degrees hotter on average. So far I am adjusting pretty well. The biggest threat we face right now is terrorism. There were threats on our position last night so we increased security. Nothing happened. But, we're still on an increased state of readiness.

I'm drinking plenty of water, taking my vitamins and taking in a lot of calories. I should be fine in that regard. I'll write for a resupply of vitamins some time later.

Morale among the soldiers is very high. But, we understand what our role is and I honestly believe that we are ready for whatever comes. We still don't have any idea how long we will be here. I'm not even going to venture a guess. I suppose it would help to have a date to focus on. But, none exists as of now. So I guess I'll be here until I come home.

How are things on the home front? Any day now I'm expecting a flood of letters from all over. ☺ I hope you have given my address to everyone.

I hope that you didn't have any problems getting my LES.[1] How are things going with "the brown car"? How's the price of gold? How is the job scene?

[1] LES: Army abbreviation for Leave and Earnings Statement, or pay stub.

17

Are you saving any money? Remember, by the time I get back I want to have $1 million. I hope that you are staying busy and taking care of yourself and not worrying about me. I'm fine.

I don't have a whole lot more to report at this time. I'll try to write frequently and I expect the same from you and everyone else. ☺

Give my best to both our families. Let everyone know I'm doing well.

Say hello to Liz and Jim. And if you see Mary Laedtke tell her hello. And tell her that I'm still hoping she doesn't have to join this big party here.

I'm trying very hard not to dwell on all the things I've left behind. I'm trying hard not to spend my time thinking of you. It is entirely too painful. Just know this – at some point I'll be back home.

I miss you more than I can possibly put into words. And I love you even more than that.

Always,
Stephen

5 SEPTEMBER, 1990

Dear Diane,

I have awakened to one more day in paradise. I'm still doing well. The first ship of our equipment should arrive sometime tomorrow. I'm sure things will be a little crazy getting all of that unscrewed and getting us moved out to an assembly area. So you may not hear from me for a few days.

How are things on the home front? I'm sure that you are doing just fine. I know that Paul is due to arrive soon. 1. Tell him hello. And tell him that he is missing all the fun. 2. So far all the intel seems to indicate that the Iraqis are hunkering down in Kuwait. And we are initially assuming a defensive posture. That could be indicative of a long stay for American troops. I still don't have any idea how long we'll be here. I probably won't have any idea for some time to come.

The plan now seems to be to put us (2-69) along the expected avenue of approach with a regiment of Marines on our right flank. It should be interesting.

I'll keep you posted on my financial needs. After you send me the initial $75 I should probably be o.k. Finance is issuing casual pay of $50 a month for those who want it. If I take one it will just come out of my LES. You shouldn't even miss it. I'm sure that you will make sound financial decisions while I'm gone. At least I hope so. ☺

Living conditions for us are not that bad. They're not that great either, but it is certainly far from being unbearable. They tell us the temperature should start to slowly decrease in early October. Any relief at all will be welcome.

I am amazingly not homesick, but I am making a conscious effort not to think about it and concentrate on the task at hand. I'll tell you what I do miss, Action!!! ☺ *Playing tennis, reading my books and laying in bed with no clothes on. I do miss other things like family and friends, but not as much as I miss you. You are my family and you are my best friend.*

I don't have much more to report. Write often and tell everyone else to write to me too. It would help me tremendously. Pictures would also be great. I promise to return everyone's letters as soon as I can.

Remember, I miss you more than I can possibly put into words, and I love you even more than that.

Always,
Stephen

DEAR DIANE

Dear Diane,

Well I've been here in The Kingdom of Saudi Arabia for 10 days and I still have not received mail from anyone. Are you sure you've given my address to people? I know I told you to wait a while before sending anything. But now I'm ready to start receiving word from the home front.

The last few days have been very busy with the first ship load of our equipment arriving. But we have nearly everything on the ground now. We should be moving out to an assembly area sometime tomorrow. It should be a welcome relief from tent city.

I've thought of a few more things that I miss: A nice cold beer, using the bathroom on a real toilet, listening to music that I want to listen to, The Capitol Gang and just hanging out at home.

I'm still holding up very well. I'm taking my vitamins and watching my calorie intake. I think I'm going to drop a few pounds regardless of what I do. But, I think I'll be able to minimize the loss. By the way you'll be happy to know that I have decided to let my mustache grow back. I know that will please you.

I still don't know how long we'll be here. The leadership seems to be hell bent on convincing everyone that this is some sort of big training exercise. As far as I'm concerned the threat of war is very real and someone should be trying to put these soldiers in that mindset.

Personally I don't see a peaceful solution to this crisis. I have not heard this through any official channels so this is just my opinion. But, by the end of October if the situation remains as is we will invade Kuwait. There will be loss of life. Hopefully, not too much.

If we decide to go into Iraq loss of life will be significant. I ask you to continue to pray for my safe return.

How are things with you? By the time this gets to you Paul will have come and gone. I hope he had a good time. Have you been able to get to Atlanta? Whenever you see Sandy and Rich give them my best. Have my mom and sister come to see you? Have you seen Mary Laedtke lately? If you do give her my best and ask her to drop me a line. How are your parents? Are they planning to come see you any time soon?

Of course I am hoping and praying for a peaceful resolution to this crisis. The thought of returning home to you is about the only thing that makes this place tolerable.

I'll write again as soon as I can. Just remember I miss you more than I can possibly put into words. And I love you more than that.

Always,
Stephen

11 SEPTEMBER, 1990
1430 HRS.

Dear Diane,

Here it is another day in paradise. Today feels a bit hotter than the past two days. But, I'm still holding up very well. The last two days have been pretty busy. We've been in the process of getting our equipment moved from here (tent city) to the forward assembly area. We've still got another ship due in tomorrow with more equipment on it. I've been placed in charge of making sure it gets unloaded and the equipment is accounted for. Then I'll move forward to join the remainder of the unit. Also, (you'll love this) I've been placed in charge of managing the battalion PX[2] facility. Yesterday I went to establish our account ($3,000) and I'll be responsible for returning that amount once the "war" is over. I see the potential for this to get out of hand unless I keep a tight rein over this stuff. Which I intend to do. But, just in case, make sure we have $3,000 set aside, so I don't have to go to jail. ☺

I still have no idea how long this adventure is going to last. I still don't see a peaceful solution to this situation, although I'm hoping and praying for one. To walk around this place though, you would not think the people are considering the threat of war a real possibility. I'm anxious to see how this whole thing plays out over the course of time. I believe that once we get established in the assembly area, if we are static for a prolonged period of time without doing anything, soldiers will become complacent and that is potentially dangerous. We'll see.

What's going on at home? How is life on good old Hampton Place? ☺ What is your job scene like? Have you had any other visitors? What's going on with the "brown car"? How are you holding up? I hope that you are not worrying about me too much. And I hope that you are taking care of yourself and enjoying yourself (but not too much ☺).

It may be a little while before you get another letter until we have some semblance of order in the assembly area. Just give my regards to everyone. Take care of yourself and be good. And remember, I miss you more than I can possibly put into words, and I love you even more than that.

Always,
Stephen

---

[2] PX: Abbreviation for post exchange.

SEPTEMBER 1990

12 SEPTEMBER, 1990
0745 HRS.

Dear Diane,

Here it is another day and I still have not received any mail from anyone. I'm not getting bummed yet but it sure would be nice to hear something from the home front sometime soon. In the last few days I have written to my mom, Anna and Larry, Barry and Wendi, Lauri and John and one potential pen pal, a high school student in Freemont, Ohio. Hopefully within a week or so someone will write back to me. And of course I have written to you. This should be the fourth or fifth letter.

Most of the battalion has moved out of tent city to the assembly area. Today should be pretty calm. I've got a couple of meetings at 0830 and 1000. But, it should be quiet until 1700 when the ship docks.

I thought of some more things that I miss. 1. Your cooking (I've had all the MRE's[3] that I can stand, but that's basically all we have). 2. Going out to dinner. 3. Crossfire. 4. Watching Catherine Crier on CNN. 5. And I'm really pissed that pro football season has started and I am missing it.

By the way, have you heard anything from Marie Bayer? For some reason she ran across my mind yesterday. If you do hear from her just give her my regards and invite her to come visit sometime.

I hope that you are not having any problems getting my pay. I don't expect that you are. But if you do just see CPT[4] K. Just remember save, save, save since I'll probably have to get a new car when I get back.

Still no word on the length of our stay. Just stay busy and try not to worry too

[3] MRE: Meal Ready to Eat, a full meal in a plastic pouch.
[4] CPT: Army abbrevation for the rank of Captain.

much. Just write soon and have others do the same. Say Hello to Liz and Jim, Sandy and Rich and Michelle Suhr. Tell her that Scott is holding up pretty well. Not much more to report at this time. I miss you and I love you.

Always,

Stephen

p.s. I've been enclosing a little of the desert in my letters to others. So now I'll do the same for you.

13 SEPTEMBER, 1990
1050 HRS.

Dear Diane,

The situation here remains basically the same. Rumors abound. I'm curious as to what kinds of things you are hearing through the wife channels. I'm thinking that maybe LTC[3] S. is informing his wife of things that he is not quite prepared to let us in on yet. Keep me posted.

The worst of the rumors is that if war does break out this will become a "short tour" for us and we will be here for a year. Believe me, just the thought of being away from you for that long is not pleasing. About the only benefit I see out of it is that you should be able to save tons of money, say at least $20,000 to $30,000. I'm serious! You could virtually live on your paycheck and save nearly all of mine. Then when I get home I could buy a new 300SX for myself. ☺ Just kidding. Anyway, even the thought of having that much money saved is not worth being away from you for that long. Really.

I've already started to think about what life will be like once we leave the Army behind. 17 May 94 will probably get here before we know it. I think a

[3] LTC: Army abbreviation for the rank of Lieutenant Colonel.

reasonable goal for us to aim for is to be nearly debt free and have invest-ments worth at least $50,000 by the time that date arrives. This figure would not include the house we're planning to buy in Atlanta or our IRA account. I think we should work toward being able to take at least 6 weeks off just to unwind from the green machine, travel to parts of the country that we've never been and prepare for a new phase of our lives. Now that's something worth working for.

It may be a little while before I'm able to write to you again. The next few days may be a little hectic. I ask that you please keep in touch. I still have not received anything from you as of this writing.

I still think of you constantly and I miss you very much. Take care of yourself and be good.

Love always,
Stephen

16 SEPTEMBER, 1990
1035 HRS.

Dear Diane,

Here it is, another day in paradise. I finally received a letter from you yester-day with $20 in it. Thank you. ☺ Please date your letters so I can track how long it is taking them to get here.

As of two days ago I became S-1 officially. S. broke the news to Scott right after the Command and Staff meeting. He seems to be taking it pretty well. I talked to him afterwards and tried to make him feel better. I think he understands.

Our assembly area is out in the middle of nowhere. My CP[5] set up is about 800 meters from a bedouin camp that has about 50 camels and 50 goats. I see them early in the morning and late in the evening. During the heat of the day they stay inside their tents. Smart.

There is nothing but desert as far as the eye can see. It's hot, it's dry, it's desolate. Soldiers are starting to become restless. It's hard not knowing when this will be over for us. But, we're holding on. As for me I'm doing fine. I'm glad that they finally moved me to a permanent position. I know I'll be a better S-1 this time than I was last time. Even though I thought I was pretty great the last time. ☺

So Sandy and Rich finally tied the knot. Be sure to congratulate them for me. I hope that you all had a good time at Six Flags. I'm glad that you are getting out and enjoying yourself. But, I don't mind admitting that I am a little jealous.

I was talking with Kevin Brau last night about what we'll do when we get back. He thought of 4 or 5 days at the Disney Resort in Orlando. If we've got the money I think it would be a blast to stay in a 1st class room in the resort and just have a leisurely mini-vacation. What do you think?

I'm glad that you gave my address to people. And I've written people. I hope to be seeing lots and lots of letters soon.

As I write this a shamal (dust storm) is going on outside. I think that it is probably a minor one but it's not at all pleasant to step outside right now.

I'm glad you're making progress on your diet. I hope it continues. Enough said. I'm glad you're paying off bills and saving money. I hope it continues. Enough said.

[5] CP: Command Post.

Regarding your general attitude leading up to my departure, I have to tell you that I was more than a little disappointed. You displayed a very selfish disposition which I found most disquieting considering the fact that I'm the one here sweating my ass off and you're back there going to Six Flags. But, I'm not upset. I don't harbor bad feelings about it. All I ask is that you get over it by the time I get home. I hope that's a reasonable request.

Not much more to report now. Just remember I miss you more than I can possibly put into words. And I love you even more than that.

Always,
Stephen

17 SEPTEMBER, 1990
0730 HRS.

Dear Diane,

I got another letter from you today. Thanks. ☺ I love so much to hear from you. I also got another letter from Marie and Gord. They have been really wonderful about writing.

For some reason my mail from this end is not getting through. I've written to them at least three times and as of their letter dated September 5 they had not received anything from me. When you talk to them please tell them that I have written. I just don't know what the problem is.

I hope that by now my letters have resumed coming to you at a high rate of consistency. I have been writing faithfully, just as you have been. By the way, who is PVT[7] Watkins?

---

[7] PVT: Army abbreviation for the rank of Private.

The prospect for potential new jobs sounds pretty good. $20 an hour at Doctor's Hospital/Agency is good money. I know that you are very talented at your profession and you deserve every penny that you make.

I hope that you got my request to send cassette tapes, GQ and Atlanta magazines, pictures and another care package. You can throw in an auto magazine also. If the brown car sells and I have to get something new I want to concentrate in the $8,000-$12,000 price range.

I'm glad that you are paying off the bills. We sure did buy a lot of nice stuff. Did you do the Atlanta housing scene with Sandy and Rich yet? It should be interesting. If we work hard over the remainder of my time in the Army we should be able to find a very, very nice home in the $150k to $200k price range (with lots of space for babies). Six of them! ☺

My current cash situation is good. There's not much of an opportunity to spend anything. I won't be taking anymore casual pay. If I need money I'll write to you for it. But I don't anticipate needing any anytime soon.

If I didn't know it before I certainly know it now: the Army is not for me long term. I've begun to ask myself seriously if taking command is really worth it. I know that there are jobs in the infamous building 4 (post HQ) that entail normal hours and no long family separations. By rights I should probably be in one of those jobs now. I've also given serious thought to resigning my commission prior to my ETS date of 17 May 94. The question that keeps coming to my mind is, why wait? I know that it's this prolonged stay in the desert that's starting to affect me. Deep down I know that we need ample time to establish stability in our finances and in our home life. Leaving the Army I know will be a tremendously stressful step. Getting an advanced degree will take time. Finding a job that pays enough to continue to support our standard of living may take time. When we do make the move I want our ducks to be lined up so that we are not proceeding half-cocked.

And we WILL make the move. Yeah!!!

By the way, did you take out that insurance policy on yourself? Just curious.

Not much more to report at this time. Your letters and the thought of being with you again is all that's keeping me going. I love you more than you realize. Then again maybe you do realize it. I sure hope so.

Always,
Stephen

18 SEPTEMBER, 1990
1800 HRS.

Dear Diane,

Right now there is a lull in the CPX[8] battle. So I decided to write you a little note. In the CPX we're still practicing a defensive scenario which I guess is still a good sign. The other day on the front page of the Stars and Stripes[9] they printed "The Scenario." It painted the picture of a 4-day, American-led attack into Iraq and Kuwait. I won't go into all the military details but the bottom line was 20,000 American dead. That's a lot in four days. We're all still hoping that it doesn't come to that.

On the lighter side, comedian Steve Martin was in the Brigade area yesterday. I didn't get to see him but some of the troops did. Some said they got some really good pictures.

Also, today I got a letter from a cousin of mine in North Carolina whom I have not seen since I was 14 or 15 years old. Pretty amazing. I was very pleasantly

---

[8] CPX: Army abbreviation for Command Post Exercise.
[9] *Stars and Stripes* is the newspaper that was distributed to military personnel in bases all over the world.

surprised. The exercise should be over by 0600 tomorrow morning. I'll write a longer letter then.

There is something you can do for me. I've enclosed an article that I wrote one night when I could not sleep. I would like for you to get it to the editor of the Columbus Ledger Enquierer for publication. If/when it runs I want you to clip it and get it framed at Framing by Michael's in the same types of frames as in my office. I plan to send the same article to Sandy and Rich, my mom and your parents to see if it can get published in any or all of their respective papers. Please keep me posted as to how it goes.

Not much more to report at this time. I love you very much.

Always,

Stephen

p.s. Right now our side is winning "the war."
p.s. Please execute my request ASAP! Thanks.

21 SEPTEMBER, 1990
1100 HRS.

Dear Diane,

Today marks exactly one month since the unit left Ft. Benning. Somehow it seems like it has been a lot longer. I'm still doing well. Now that I am S-1 I am a lot busier than I used to be, which is fine with me. It helps the time pass faster. I've been marking days off my little Merchants Bank calendar. Within the last week I've been so wrapped up doing that I let three days pass before I marked them off. It sure would be nice if three days could pass at a time all the time.

I still have no idea when we'll return. Everyone seems to be stuck on the figure 180 days (6 months). I suppose that would be semi-acceptable. But if we continue to just sit here without doing anything, I think they should pull us out much sooner.

As each day passes we get closer and closer to reverting back to complete admin mode. In another 30 days it will be like we were just picked up at Ft. Benning and brought here. This is not necessarily bad except for: 1. conditions are austere in that we are not operating out of buildings. 2. We're not going home every night. 3. We don't have weekends and it is generally not very pleasant here. Aside from that...

By the way, I've thought of some more things that I miss. 1. Shooting pool. 2. Wearing my wedding band. 3. Being able to sleep in at least one day a week and 4. Action!!! I probably mentioned action in my first letter. Well I miss it a little more now. ☺ It will probably get worse as time goes on.

I received another letter from you a few days ago. Thanks. Keep them coming. Tell Christine Petersen that I appreciate her concern. If you send me their address I'll drop them a line. I also got two letters from your sister Marie. They were both very cheerful and made me smile. I'll write to her ASAP!

I think that it would be very nice if you visited my mom in October. I'm sure she would appreciate it. Tell her I'm fine. Also, when in Savannah say hi to Barry and Jo, Tom and Betsy, Billy and anyone else you happen to run into.

A few other things: Continue to send money in small increments. I'm sure I'll get around to spending it sometime. Georgia taxes should not show up on my LES until EOM[10] September. I'm glad you've gotten inquiries about the car. Maybe it will sell soon.

---

[10] EOM: Army abbreviation for End of Month.

The weather seems to be getting a little cooler, which is welcome relief. I have not completed shooting the first roll of film yet, but I'll send it when I do.
I don't have much more to report at this time. Just continue to be strong and before you know it we'll be together again.

Take care of yourself and be good. I love you more than anything. Even brussell sprouts. ☺

Always,
Stephen

p.s. If you send a care package, make sure it includes pogey bait and razor blades.

22 SEPTEMBER, 1990
1015 HRS.

Dear Diane,

Another day in paradise. Last night we moved from our location to another location. Later today we are moving again. 7 -10 days from now we may be moving again. Apparently there is some sort of squabble going on between the Army and the Marine Corps over who occupies what spot. So far the Army is losing.

I've been thinking a lot about babies lately and have come to no conclusions yet. I've thought about all the reasons that I married you. One of the big ones is that I wanted you to be the mother of my children. I know that you have good values and I know that the babies would love you. ☺ I'm not opposed to the idea of adoption. But, I'm starting to feel like years from now we may regret not at least trying to have one baby of our own.

I've considered what it might be like for our child to grow up with inter-racial parents. And I'm sure instances will arise when our child would be faced with dealing with racial slurs. However, I would hope that between the two of us we could provide enough love and support to keep our child on an even keel.

I also know what's involved with trying to make this happen. I know that time is in essence running out. I know that going through the surgical procedure would be hard on you. I don't necessarily want that.

I've also considered the fact that a baby, either biological or adopted, would change our whole life. We've been married for over three years and we've had a lot of fun together. But, somehow it just doesn't seem that we've spent a lot of time together. I know it's selfish, but I just don't know if I am ready to share you with a baby yet. I want to keep you for myself for a while longer.

I guess the bottom line is that I'm still very confused. If you have strong feelings about this subject, please let me know how you feel one way or the other. It would help me tremendously.

Not much more to report at this time. I think of you often. Continue to hold down the fort until I return. And take care of yourself.

Love,
Stephen

p.s. When you send a care package, please enclose one or two electric razors and some batteries.

DEAR DIANE

Dear Diane,

Another day in paradise. Believe it or not the temperature is starting to drop. The daytime highs are getting up only to about 103 degrees. That's a big difference from 112 degrees and it is a welcome relief.

I got your care package a couple of days ago. Thanks a lot. It really made me feel good. It was dated 13 September which means it's taking about 10 days for mail to get over here. The next time you send one, please enclose a few cassette tapes for me to listen to. No more than five or six. No special request. You know what I like.

So far I have not used the cassette recorder that you bought for me. I'm sorry. I just have not had the chance to steady myself enough to talk into the thing. It's just easier for me to write. I know you would like to hear my voice just as I would like to hear yours. I'll make every effort to get a tape out to you as soon as possible. Please do the same.

I guess you've received the "baby letter" by now. I really would like to know what you really think regarding all of that. It would help me to know and it would settle me down on that particular issue.

So what's going on back home? Have you done anything fun lately? How is work? Has the brown car sold yet? Have you had anymore visitors? Be sure to keep me posted.

Yesterday the staff had a briefing from the 24th Infantry Division Commander (two stars). He basically told us that he did not know how things were going to turn out i.e.; if we would continue to sit here or if we would invade Kuwait. He said that the next 30-90 days would be critical and that by the end of a 90-day period the picture should be much clearer. He said that if we did go to war we would win decisively in about 7 days. He did not feel that the Iraqi Army would invade Saudi Arabia. He did not feel that American units would rotate on a periodic basis. He felt that if and when and when troops were sent back to the U.S., the 24th ID (plus the 197th) would be one of the last units to leave as opposed to being one of the first. He made it clear that he was not volunteering for war but that if we were called upon we would execute. All of this boils down to the fact that we will probably be here "a good long time." I don't know what that translates to in months, but I'd say 6-12 is a pretty good guess. Of course, he did stress that these remarks represented his own personal opinions, nothing more. And that he was hoping for a speedy resolution and return home just like everyone else. So much for that.

It is imperative during this time, however long it is, that we keep the lines of communication open between us. Please let me know how you feel about things so that we don't lose the bond between us. I trust you to do all the right things for the two of us.

After all, we are a family. My love for you grows stronger with each passing day. And it's the knowledge of that love that will sustain me through whatever comes. Take care of yourself and be good.

Always,
Stephen

p.s. Still have not received letters from anyone other than you and Marie. But, I'm still looking for a whole lot. ☺

DEAR DIANE

Dear Diane,

Another day in paradise. October 1 is almost upon me. To me that signifies sort of a demarcation point. I know that forces are continuing to come in. Everything should be here by about 1 November. Then somebody is going to have to make a big decision.

We'll see. Who knows? Maybe the air embargo will force Iraq to do something stupid. Or maybe the Iraqi people will rise up and kill Hussein. That would be the best of all possibilities. But, I don't think it is likely.

Mail is starting to roll in now. Thanks for giving "everyone" my address. In recent days I've received letters from JD, Joyce Peter, your parents and Steve Jackson in Germany. JD also sent me a care package which I thought was very nice.

I've started to settle into my role as S-1. At first it seemed like I was getting bogged down in a lot of bullshit, which I was. One night I pulled S. aside after the command and staff meeting and told him straight out that I did not think other people (namely the CSM[11]) were doing their jobs. He said he would take care of it. Since then some of the extraneous bullshit has been relieved and I can concentrate on doing my job.

I've been doing some thinking. I know that whenever I get home we'll do some fun travel things together. But, I've got an idea for our fifth wedding anniversary. Hong Kong! Rather than spending big bucks on a 300SX ☺ we could take a super vacation. Something to think about.

Speaking of spending money, I think you should start shopping around for a

---

[11] CSM: Army abbreviation for Command Sergeant Major.

computer. Seriously! I've come to the conclusion that my computer skills suck. Having one at home would go a long way toward helping. If you should find a good deal and buy one before I get home, I ask that you not set it up in my office (more specifically on my desk). I just don't want the look of the room destroyed by a hulking computer. No more money matters for now. I know that you are doing good things.

How is everyone on that end? I kinda feel sorry for Mary L. being in limbo. I really hope that she doesn't have to come here. Although I must say that the few women that I've had dealings with out here seem to be giving a good account of themselves. There is one who works in Brigade S-1 who seems to be okay. We've just recently got 2 female medics attached to us. They seem to be holding their own. But I'm most impressed with a transportation Captain that works in Brigade S-4. Her name is Kerri Gum. She has probably worked the hardest of anyone during the last 20-30 days getting us over here. I know that she had to be in maximum overdrive. But, every time I saw her she seemed to be in complete control. Sort of like me. ☺ Anyway, I know that you think I'm a chauvinist. I just wanted to let you know that I am trying to be better about that in recognizing people who do the job regardless of gender.

A few more things. If my Atlanta magazine subscription has kicked in, how about sending those to me? Also a few more razor blades would be nice. You can send GQ also.

Not much more to report at this time. Thanks so much for your volume of letters. I can't begin to tell you how much it means for me to hear from you. My love for you grows stronger with each passing day. Take care of yourself and be good.

Love,
Stephen

DEAR DIANE

Dear Diane,

I just got another one of your letters. Thanks. You're doing a wonderful job writing. I also got a letter from my sister yesterday. It makes me a little sad. I hope that she and my mom are really o.k.

FYI I still have not received the $50 or the AT&T card that you sent. They may be just held up. Then again, they may have swiped it. We are getting reports that some of the mail is being censored. It might be wise to put a trace on it.

Well, I suppose I'll get ready for another day. I've got a staff briefing with the Colonel at 0700. It should be o.k.

Thanks again for your continued love and support. Believe it or not I can feel your good vibes all the way from Columbus. Take care of yourself and be good.

Love always,
Stephen

three

OCTOBER 1990

Waiting...

When the seemingly simple joys are removed from life, it's amazing how you come to miss them. These are the parts that happen as a matter of routine and detail between the monumental events, the mortar between the foundation of bigger milestone moments. Of course, I am talking about watching football.

As the deployment continued I was aching for the professional football season. My college alma mater, Armstrong State College in Savannah, Georgia, didn't have a football team. So, while I was a fan of the collegiate game I was never really into it. The NFL was a different matter altogether. I loved it.

Growing up, I played plenty of sandlot and street football. I was an average player, and I could usually take a hit fairly well. But, I was always pretty skinny, so I never played in any organized leagues. I really wish I had, in spite of my size. Maybe that's why I like the NFL so such. It's the game I love being played at the highest level, and I enjoy the speed and the contact.

In fact, my Sundays during the fall were set. In the mornings, I would watch the talking heads ("Meet the Press," "This Week with David Brinkley," etc.) and football in the afternoons. To me that was just about a perfect day. However, the harmony of my fall Sundays was shattered as a result of this deployment, and I missed it desperately.

There were also other things (some might say more important things) that I missed. Things like sex. Yes, I said it! Keep in mind that Diane and I had been married for a little over three years and I was only in my mid-20's when I was deployed. Enough said.

I also missed drinking beer, and a little Scotch, too. My boys and I did our share of damage, and had lots of fun in the process. I also remember getting tipsy with my landlord at my first apartment in Germany. His English was minimal and my German was almost non-existent. Yet, we found a way to commune and bond as we shared a universal language with plenty of Kulmbacher Pils serving as the catalyst.

But, as I eventually discovered, Saudi Arabia is a Muslim country. There was no alcohol of any kind anywhere in sight. It's not allowed anywhere. I don't remember how I learned about this for the first time, but I can say it was disappointing news, to say the least.

Let me emphasize that I don't mean to make light of such things. And I certainly don't want to give the impression that I had some sort of drinking problem. The point I'm making is that we come to take for granted the routines that define our lives – the habits and activities that, mundane as they seem, keep us balanced and grounded and give us comfort and joy. And once I found myself without those daily comforts that I'd come to take for granted, it would take some time to adapt.

But difficult as it was, I was determined to get used to my new normal in the Arabian Desert. In fact, as a result of training and conditioning, soldiers are especially good at adapting. Still, I knew I had a tough road ahead – especially without the sex, Sunday football and the Scotch I loved so much.

On the home front, while I knew Diane missed me, I really didn't worry about how she was holding up at this point. I've always admired how strong she is emotionally, and I knew she had her family and work to keep her busy. At the time, she was working for the military too, as a civilian charge nurse in the ICU[12] at Martin Army Hospital at Fort Benning. It was a source of pride for me that, like me, she was also working for the good of our country.

She was also becoming quite close friends with a woman named Michelle Suhr. Michelle was a fellow officer's wife – in fact, her husband, Scott, and I were in the same battalion – and she and Diane depended on each other for support and companionship. Michelle was in charge

---

[12] ICU: Abbreviation for Intensive Care Unit.

of welcoming new officers' wives to the battalion, and about two weeks after we arrived in Fort Benning, she showed up at our apartment and introduced herself with a casserole and a bottle of tequila. She and Diane spent plenty of evenings together eating chips and salsa and drinking high-quality tequila.

Knowing that Diane had someone to rely on was extremely comforting to me – especially as I started to miss the comforts of home so much.

2 OCTOBER, 1990
0745 HRS.

Dear Diane,

Another day in paradise. It's been 40 days since we left Ft. Benning. How are you holding up? I know that you're doing just fine. I'm still hanging in there like everyone else. Nobody knows what the future holds.

Today was a good mail day. I got letters from Marie and Gord, Anna and Larry, Sandy and Joyce Peter. Anna and Larry sent me three pictures of Joanna and Little Larry. I can't believe how fast they are growing up. They will both be graduating from college before we know it.

I'm glad that you find my list of things that I miss amusing. It would probably be interesting seeing a compilation of that list by the time I return, so here are a few more items: 1. Going out dancing. 2. Courvoisier (only occasionally). 3. Cigars (only occasionally, although I have been able to smoke a few out here). 4. Wearing my wedding band. 5. Wearing my Rolex and diamond ring and 6. Action!!! You know what they say. A day without action is like a day without sunshine. ☺

So what's going on at home? How are our Scudder funds doing? I hope that you're still hanging in there at work.

DEAR DIANE

I got a copy of my EOM September LES. Georgia State taxes were quite a bite. Plus the one exemption made a difference. Hopefully it will save us a little grief at tax time. We've got to come up with a way to save on taxes.

It is my feeling that the next 40 days will be critical. All of the American forces coming into the region should be here by the end of the month. Once they have a week or two to settle in I see no reason why we should not go on the offensive if the situation is still the same. I think that the soldiers are tired of just sitting around. Personally, I'm staying fairly busy, which is good because it helps the time go by faster. But I think a combination of the heat and the boredom is making the "average Joe" a little stir crazy.

By the way, I've come to the conclusion that MAJ[13] R. is a fucking moron. I can tell that our relationship won't be harmonious. I really don't care. I know that I am doing a good job. And I know that S. is impressed with my work and trusts my judgement. That's all that matters.

When you talk to people on the phone, please tell them that I am receiving their letters and I am extremely grateful for their sentiments. And I will return letters to them. Every single one of them.

As for you, I can't begin to thank you enough for your continued love and support. You are the most wonderful wife a man could ever have. You are the best friend anyone could ever hope to have. And I appreciate you very much. Take care of yourself and be good.

Love always,
Stephen

p.s. Just out of curiosity, have you heard anything out of Maria Mowbray lately?

---

[13] MAJ: Army abbreviation for the rank of Major.

Dear Honey Buns (Oh, that's me ☺,)

Another day in paradise. I got your letter of 23 Sept. Thanks so much for en-closing the letter from Nina. When all of this is over we'll have to make plans to visit them or have them visit us. That would be fun. I really like them both.

How are you holding up? I know that you are doing fine. I sincerely hope that you find a work situation that makes you happy. Work represents such a big part of people's lives. If that aspect is unpleasant to the point of being almost intolerable then it's simply not worth it to continue. Since we've been married, I know that you have been a slave to the "green machine" regarding your employment. I wish there was something more that I could do to help the situation. I just want you to be happy.

The letter from my grandmother was nice. Regarding their donation request for the church, I'll leave the decision totally up to you.

When you see Sandy and Rich tell them congrats for me. I just recently got a note from Sandy which told me about the fun things you guys did in Atlanta. I'm glad that you all had a good time. I'll write to her as soon as possible. Be sure to thank Marie and Gord for their supportive letters. Their kindness has been wonderful. I will write to them again soon.

The situation for us remains basically the same. No real need to worry yet. My gut feeling is that the month of November will be critical. This stalemate cannot go on forever. Something has to give. I just hope that the bloodshed is minimal, preferably zero.

In some ways you may be starting to get more like me. I hope that is a trend that does not continue. The things that I love about you the most are some of the things where we are the most different. And while I may not aspire to some of those qualities, I do respect them and love and respect you for holding onto them.

Regarding the stuff that people want to put in care packages: MUNCHIES!!! I need something to augment this wonderful Army cuisine that I've been enjoying. By the way, there is something else that I miss. Nice salads with nice dressing. You can add that to the list.

Please give everyone concerned my very best. Let them know that SRB is hanging in there. Tell them to continue to pray for peace and to keep those letters coming. Take care of yourself and be good.

Love always,
Stephen

6 OCTOBER, 1990
0930 HRS.

Dear Diane,

I got your letter of Sept 12 today. Enclosed was the $50 and the AT&T card. Thanks! It is always good to hear from you. It's been really great hearing from other people, too. I can't begin to thank you enough for getting my address out to everyone. I've really collected a nice stack of letters. But, I look forward to hearing from you most of all. You are the best part of my life. I try very hard not to think about how much I miss you. It hurts too much.

I also got the letter with the California pictures in it. It did bring back fond memories. We really did have a good time. The thought of having good times like that again is what keeps me going.

Although nothing has been put out officially, I'm still looking for an allied (American) offensive sometime in November. The situation as it stands now cannot continue. Hussein cannot stay in Kuwait and American soldiers cannot sit on the ground here doing nothing indefinitely. I continue to pray for peace but I just don't know if it is going to happen.

Meanwhile we sit here and wait. And the bullshit continues to mount. Being here would not be half as bad if many of the stupid requirements went away. At this time, we seem to be heading toward creating a Ft. Benning Middle East rather than getting these soldiers in the mindset of killing people and possibly dying. Instead of practicing things as we would do them in war we seem to be trying to create as many administrative requirements as possible. I wish someone would make up their minds. Oh, by the way, MAJ R. is still a moron.

If shooting does start soon I'll be sure to carry my "lucky" picture of us with me. It got me safely through airborne school. I expect it to get me safely through combat. I absolutely refuse to believe that I will never see you again. I'll be back. You can count on that. ☺

Not much more to report at this time. I love you very much. Take care and be good.

Always,
Stephen

p.s. The letter that I got from West Point is very interesting. I'm not giving it serious consideration. I think we both know what I really want to do. Anyway, it is interesting.

DEAR DIANE

7 OCTOBER, 1990
1320 HRS.

Dear Diane,

Another day in paradise. The weather is now beginning to get a little cooler. The nights and early mornings are actually quite pleasant. But the daytime highs still reach into the 90's. Even so, it is a lot more bearable than 110 degrees.

LTC S. gave us a brief last night about how forces will ultimately be arranged probably by the end of the month. I can't go into any details except to say that it is still a defensive scenario. I still believe that somebody somewhere has got to be making plans for offensive operations. They are just keeping it very quiet. Enough of this.

How are things on the home front? I'm sure that it is very easy keeping the apartment neat with me not around. I guess I was an OINK! OINK! Maybe by the time I get back I'll be a piglet. ☺

Needless to say, I'm still missing you very much. Especially with no clothes on. ☺ I hope you are continuing to take care of yourself. And I hope that you are managing to have some fun.

I guess by now Sandy and Rich are married. I hope they are doing well. I'm glad that lots of people are calling you to show their support. It is nice to have good friends. I hope to be able to thank all of them in person when I get out of here.

I guess Mary Laedtke has deployed by now. If you have an APO[14] address for her please send it. I seriously doubt that I'll be able to see her while we're here. But at least we could write to each other.

How's work? I know… a potentially sore subject. But I've been thinking about how you have said that you wanted to do some type of work for an insurance company.

---

[14] APO: Abbreviation for Army Post Office.

Well, American Family Life HQ is right in Columbus. Who knows? With your experience and wonderful personality you might be able to find a good position that pays good money. Remember, we have to make money for the family. Think about it.

Mail flow lately has been very good. Right now I owe letters to Anna and Larry, J.D., and Gord and Marie. But, it seems that every time I sit down to write, the one person that I want to communicate with is you. I plan to send out return letters to them tomorrow.

Sometimes when I have time to think I remember how we met and all of the things that we have gone through. I really believe that we are a good team. And I love you more now than ever. If you continue to be a sweet and wonderful person I may extend our marriage from 75 years to 85 or 90. ☺ Continue to be strong. Take care of yourself and be good.

Love always,
Stephen

9 OCTOBER, 1990
1100 HRS.

Dear Diane,

Another day in paradise. We got bad news last night at the Command and Staff meeting. It seems there was a fire at the Division Postal facility. 40% of the mail was burned. At this point there is no way of knowing what or whose mail was destroyed. I can tell you this much, it has not done anything for troop morale, which is already beginning to slide into the toilet. We don't even know if it was incoming mail or outgoing mail. It really sucks. I did get letters from Liz and Jim and your sister Karen the other day. It was really nice to hear from them. But, I have received nothing else since then.

We have not heard any official word yet but I am still convinced that this conflict will only be resolved through fighting. I honestly believe that the U.S. can do what has to be done while keeping American casualties at a minimum. It all depends on how we choose to execute. We'll see.

So what's the scoop with the brown car? I really won't be disappointed if it does not sell. After all the money that we have spent on it, it should be fine for a long time. I would personally have no problem driving that car until yours is paid off. Avoiding two car payments is a good objective. However, if you can get what you are asking in cold hard cash then by all means sell it.

What have you found out about taxes? How's work? I am genuinely concerned about your job satisfaction. Has anyone else come to visit you? Have you been able to have some fun? I hope so. I really do care about your well being.

I'm still hanging in there. Mornings are the hardest time of the day. Waking up to the realization that I am still here is less than pleasing. But, I get over it rather quickly and get on with whatever I've got going that day.

I can't begin to tell you how much I miss you. It's not just ACTION. Although we do have good action. ☺ But, what I miss the most is just being around you. When I get back I want to spend as much time with you as possible.

About the only shows on TV that I'm really missing (besides the ones I've previously mentioned) are LA Law, Equal Justice and Thirtysomething. Hopefully I will be home in time to catch the reruns.

Not much more to report at this time. I'll let you know about the mail situation as I get more information. I love you so much. Take care and be good.

Always,
Stephen

11 OCTOBER, 1990
1200 HRS.

Dear Diane,

Another day in paradise. It seems that the mail is still very fucked up. They are still trying to sort things out after that recent fire that burned a bunch of it. Needless to say, this situation is not doing anything for troop morale.

More bad news blew in yesterday. It seems that the ADC-M[15] (one star) was in the area yesterday to visit and talk to troops. In addition to spreading the good news of no schools, no leave and no chance for EM'S[16] to gain promotion points, he basically told soldiers to plan on staying here for one year. That bit of knowledge did nothing for morale either. I don't know if that is true or not. Maybe he is just playing the role of division doomsayer so that when we leave earlier everyone will think we caught a break. I just don't know. I've got to tell you that the prospect of not seeing you for a year makes me very sad. I'll survive. We'll survive because we have to. The only consolation that could be derived from that situation (if it happens) is that there are thousands of others who will be going through the same thing.

I've decided that if I am going to be here for awhile there is no reason why my library should not continue to grow. I've enclosed a list of books that I want you to get for me. The paperbacks I want you to send to me so I can read them. The hardbacks I want you to buy and put them on the shelves. Don't worry about trying to send all the paperbacks at once. It may take a while to gather them. As I think of more books that I want, I'll send them to you. Additionally, I have ordered some books to be sent to our address. They will be coming from The History Book Club of Camp Hill, PA. I'm only getting a total of 4 books. Three should be $1 each. The fourth one should be about $20 plus S&H. After book #4 arrives, cancel. Taking care of these books is a small thing but it will mean so much to me.

---

[15] ADC-M: Army abbreviation for the Assistant Division Commander for Maneuver.
[16] EM: Army abbreviation for enlisted men.

DEAR DIANE

I'm still doing fine. The days seem to be going faster. It seems like just yesterday it was Oct 1. Let's hope the trend continues.

I have made another decision. I have decided that I not only love you... I need you. Yes, I NEED YOU. I know that I present this Mr. Independent front a lot. Well, it's just a front. I'm sure that you probably already know that, but I wanted you to get it from me. You are the most important thing in my life. And I can't begin to imagine what my life would be without you.

I'll continue to hang in there for however long it takes. My love for you grows stronger with each passing day. Take care and be good.

Always,
Stephen

15 OCTOBER, 1990
1210 HRS.

Dear Diane,

Day before yesterday was a good mail day. I got 4 letters from you plus 1 from Liz-ella and La-poon-tang and one from Marie and Gord. Today I got another letter from you and one from Ann and Ken in Ohio. They enclosed two beautiful pictures of Katherine. Of course the letters were a little crisp around the edges, results of the fire that I wrote you about. I don't know if anything that anyone sent to me was completely destroyed. I may never know.

The tone of your letters is good. You seem to be holding up very well. I'm glad. I know that you will be alright. I got your response to the baby letter. I can be happy with adopted children. As long as they know that we both love them I'm sure that they will be o.k.

OCTOBER 1990

I'm glad that you decided against taking in a boarder. You just can't tell about some people or the people that they choose to hang out with. Besides, I would think that privacy would be of a very high premium now.

I heard about at least part of your visit to Savannah from one of the soldiers out here, SGT[17] William Reeves. It seems he and his dad know Tom and Betsy Kohler. Apparently, SGT Reeves had talked to his father on the phone and he told him that he met you. What a small world. You may recall that SGT Reeves was in A Company 1-69 when I was XO.[18]

How are Tom and Betsy and baby? I hope they are fine. I don't have their address. I sure would love to be able to write them.

So, have you felt the need to purchase a vibrator yet? I personally don't believe that you would resort to that, but then again... I MISS ACTION!!! Last night I had a dream about you. But the things I dreamed about doing with you probably should not be written here (the mail censors might freak out). Let's just say when I get back we should spend at least the first 48 hours in bed continuously. Maybe longer. ☺

F. (MAJ R.) and I are doing better. He's still a moron, but I've figured out how to keep him from getting his panties in an uproar. I know what I'm doing. He knows I know what I'm doing. So I just continue to march and he does not bother me.

Did Mary L. ever deploy? Just curious. Is James La-poon still coming to the 24th ID? Has Liz found a job? Do we still have the brown car?

I'm glad to know that our Global fund is doing well. I've got a feeling that it's going to make a lot of money over the next 10 years. I hope that you do the Atlanta housing recon with Sandy and Rich. It would probably give us a

---

[17] SGT: Army abbreviation for the rank of Sergeant.
[18] XO: Army abbreviation for Executive Officer.

good idea for when we're in that housing market. I know that you are doing well with finances. Having the bills paid off will be nice. We did purchase a lot of stuff. Nice stuff.

I know that our start in Columbus was not the smoothest. About the only benefit I see in this prolonged separation is the fact that I think we will appreciate each other more.

This will be good as we gear up toward leaving the "green machine" behind and starting a new aspect of our lives together.

I love you very much.

> *Always,*
> *Stephen*

p.s. It's time for another care package. Whatever you want to send is fine. Kool Aid (pre-sweetened) would be great.

15 OCTOBER, 1990
1815 HRS

Dear Diane,

I thought I would drop you another line today. I'm sitting here getting ready to go to my nightly Command and Staff meeting at 1900 hrs. We seem to be the only battalion in the Brigade that holds one of these things every single night. It's stupid. Some of us staff officer types are getting fed up. One night soon instead of going to the meeting we're going to send all of our NCO'S[19]. We'll see if the higher ups get the message.

---

[19] NCO: Army abbreviation for non commissioned officers.

OCTOBER 1990

FYI I'm no longer the PX officer. I did some slick maneuvering and wiggled my way out of it. My liability is absolutely 0. I still have oversight responsibility to make sure things run smoothly. But, I am not signed for anything. Yeah!

If Michelle has not told you already, Scott is a Platoon leader in A Company now. He seems very happy. I think he will do a good job. I'll keep him in mind as a future XO for when I take command. But, don't let that get out.

16 OCTOBER, 1990
0630 HRS.

I've been up for awhile. Tomorrow we start a Command Post Exercise (CPX) to practice how we will operate in case we go to war. I didn't dream about you last night. It's probably a good thing. It's so frustrating not being able to touch you. I miss you so much.

I got two more letters from you this morning. Thanks so much. You are really doing a wonderful job in writing. It means everything to hear from you. For me, sitting down to write to you is as important as getting letters from you. It is the only means I have of communicating and it offers me an escape outlet other than sleeping.

Because of the CPX, the next three days may not afford me the opportunity to write to you. But I'll resume as soon as the exercise is over.

I'm still doing fine. Yes, I'm sick of MRE's. We've started getting T-rations twice a day, which is a slight cut above MRE's but it is a little improvement. You don't need to send any videotapes. I'll just wait until I return. By the way, thanks for taping Kennedy-Nixon. That gives me something else to look forward to.

I'll give some thought to a Christmas wish list. I'll let you know. How are things back there? How is CPT K. doing in your opinion? I can tell you that LTC S. is not pleased at all with his performance. He asked me to draft a nasty-gram to send to him to express his displeasure. It should probably get to him about the time this letter gets to you.

I'm still working on the first roll of film. I'm kind of leery about sending it back through the mail. The battalion PA[20] had a couple rolls of film confiscated by someone before it reached his wife back home. However, Ann and Ken did request a picture of me.

When I finally get done I guess I'll chance it and send it to you for development. Then you can distribute the pictures as you see fit.

I understand George Michael has a new CD out called Listen Without Prejudice. It's supposed to be pretty good. How about picking it up and making a tape to send. I hope that you got my previous request for tapes and my book request (paperback only should be sent here).

Not much more to report at this time. We're all sitting around seemingly waiting for the other shoe to drop. We are all still hoping and praying for peace of course. We'll just see what happens. The thought of one day being with you again is about the only thing that keeps me going. My love and affection grows stronger with each passing day. Take care and be good.

Always,
Stephen

p.s. If you get some pictures during your travels, please send some.

---

[20] PA: Army abbreviation for Physician's Assistant.

20 OCTOBER, 1990
1415 HRS.

Dear Diane,

Tomorrow marks day 60 of our deployment. I'm still holding steady. I've settled into a groove. Now I'm just taking it one day at a time. I'm trying to stop
speculating on how long we'll be here or if we'll go to war or not. Rumors are
rampant. Most of them fall on the favorable side. But I won't even write any
of them down for fear of getting your hopes up unnecessarily. I'm fighting
the urge of placing any credence at all into any of this. But, I'm only human.

I hope that the letter containing my article "Perspectives" has arrived. I'm
curious to see if it in fact will be printed. I've also decided to send a copy to
Larry and Anna for publication in the Gainesville paper. I may even send a
copy to Barry and Wendi. I may as well cover the county.

With regard to buying the vibrator, get one if you feel you must. I only have
two requests. 1. Don't injure yourself with that thing. 2. Don't get one that's
too big. I wouldn't want to have to compete with that thing when I get back.
☺ Whenever I do get back, all I can say is that you better be READY! The
dreams that I have been having lately have been pretty WILD!

I suppose that Mary L. is somewhere in theater[21] by now. I'm kind of surprised
that she never wrote. Anyway, I'm glad that you got to spend time together.
I'm glad that Michael shoots pool. I know that you will enjoy that. Just don't
get too good.

In your last letter you alluded to the fact that you were a little worried about
Ken. What did you mean? I hope that he is not in any trouble. Lord knows my
mom has enough to worry about.

---

[21] "In theater" is a common military phrase that means the area of operations; in other
words, where a unit is located and/or war is taking place.

I'm surprised you did not elaborate more on your time in Savannah. Maybe there is more to come in letters that will cross this one in the mail. I don't have Tom and Betsy's address. Please send.

Another set of DCU's[22] would be great! Just make sure you get my nametag, US Army, Captain's bars, armor branch insignia, airborne wings, 197th patch and US flag sewn on. You can also send a set of polypropylene underwear. Mornings are cool. Regarding other care package requests, I have nothing specific. You know me. Send stuff you think I would like. I trust you.

Not much more to report at this time. Just keep those letters coming. You are doing a terrific job. I love you very much. Take care and be good.

Always,
Stephen

p.s. Also enclosed is a letter that I wrote a while back. It came back to me because I sent it to 6561 Hampton Way El Paso, TX. I must have got confused in my addressing. Oh well!

24 OCTOBER, 1990
0745 HRS.

Dear Diane,

It's been a few days since I've written to you. Sorry. But, it does not mean that I have not been writing at all. Within a few days of receipt of this letter the ladies of 2-69 should be receiving a letter from the Colonel. I'll give you three guesses as to who the ghost writer was. In recent days I've also returned letters from other people. Mail is still fucked up. I got your letter dated 7 October yesterday. I got your letter from 10 October about three days prior to

[22] DCU: Army abbreviation for Desert Camouflage Uniforms.

that. I don't know if the postal system will ever get its act together.

Anyway, I am still doing fine. I'm missing you very much but I'm still holding on. Lately it has been difficult to gauge how events are shaping up on the diplomatic front. All of us are trying to maintain a positive outlook as the days roll on. The thought of one day seeing your cute little face (among other cute things) is the only thing that's keeping me going.

Last Sunday the officers played a tackle football game which was a lot of fun. I played quarterback most of the time for our side. I played fairly well but I did take one or two good shots. I did not get hurt though. I think people are surprised by how tough I am despite my small size. My offensive line sucked. If I could have got an additional 2-3 seconds in the pocket when I dropped back to pass we would have kicked their ass. But we lost 12–0. Also, the Colonel was on the other team and I think a lot of our guys were afraid to stick him. MAJ T. was on our side. The guys on the other team were not afraid to hit him. In fact they were lowering the boom on him. It was kind of amusing. My body was a little sore the next day. But it felt GOOD!

At this point I want you to know that I am very proud of you. I'm proud of the way that you're holding things together at home. But, I knew that you would. I know that you took care of yourself before you met me and it was just a matter of readjusting. I know that you are doing good things with the money and I want you to have fun.

How is the diet going? It probably helps not having me there to pressure you. Of course, regardless of what you look like, I'm going to attack you when I get home. ☺ Not much more to report at this time. I'll continue to write as often as I can. Give everyone my best. Take care and be good.

Love,

Stephen

DEAR DIANE

25 OCTOBER, 1990
0640 HRS.

Dear Diane,

Another day in paradise. I woke up thinking about you. Not about sex. I just thought about how nice it would be just to be with you. I miss snuggling with you in bed and I miss talking to you. But, I'm still holding on. Somehow it seems to be getting a little easier. It really helps to know that you are holding things together. One day at a time is how I'm taking it now. That's about all I can do.

Do we still own the brown car? If so it might help to be a little more flexible on the asking price. It might be smart to be willing to take $2,000. However, if by the time you receive this letter you have sold it for the asking price then you were smart to do so.

I just got this morning's mail. I got another sweet letter from you. Thanks. You have really been wonderful. It was dated 16 October. I'm still looking for an APO address for Mary L. and my brother Tony. I'm glad that you and Mary and Mike have become friends. I knew that you would like each other. I guess you Wisconsin people have to stick together. Speaking of which, I just got a nice letter from Rita Olsen. It was very sweet. I will write back ASAP!

Universal news flash. MAJ "Moron" R. just made the LTC list below the zone.[23] Can you believe it? If he is regarded as one of the Army's future stars I know that my days in the green machine are numbered. As soon as I get back I'm going to start a master's degree program. I've decided to get it in Human Resources Management. Such a degree I feel would make my options in the civilian world a little greater, and me a lot more marketable. I'll probably be looking at two years of hard work. But I know that in the long run it will be

---

[23] "Below the zone" means ahead of one's peers.

worth it. Which reminds me, I've got some info around the house regarding an HRM degree program offered by Troy State University. I think it is in the file cabinet. Please send ASAP.

Still no word on when we might be leaving. No word on if we are going to attack. As I have stated before, I have finished speculating. We are just waiting to see what happens. I hope that my article arrived. I think it is positive and may be somewhat of a comfort to those who read it, if it is printed.

I'll have to cut this short. I just got a call over the radio. Another fire that has to be put out. It requires my immediate presence at the Brigade ALOC (Administration and Logistics Operations Center). This entails a 15-mile ride on an unpaved, bumpy desert road. Oh well.

You are in my thoughts constantly. My love grows stronger with each passing day. I'll just be glad when all of this is over so we can get on with the rest of our lives.

Love,

Stephen

26 OCTOBER, 1990
0730 HRS.

Dear Diane,

I got another letter from you today. Thanks! I'm glad to know that you are having more fun. I'm sure dinner at Shogun III with Mary and Mike was a good time for you. I'm glad you've all become friends.

Thanks in advance for the care package that you have sent. I hope you sent lots of munchies. Please include my GQ magazines from now on. I am willing to take the chance of them getting through. Just be careful how you label the box. Don't be too explicit about the contents and maybe they will just leave it alone.

I have another book request. The book is entitled TREVAYNE by Robert Ludlum. I'm reading the paperback right now. I'd like for you to get the hardback for me. It was originally published in 1973, so you will have to check at a used book store. Also, on the original, Robert Ludlum used a pen name which was Johnathan Ryder. As the other books that I have requested come in, just stack them in the closet off my office rather than putting them on the shelves. I'll sort through them when I get home. Thanks!

It sounds like you are becoming a smart investor re: the gold fund. You seem to be on top of things. Other financial matters to consider:

1. *The CD matures around Jan. 18. Interest should be around $350. If you have the money, add another $1,650 and purchase another 6 month CD for $12,000. If $1,650 is too much, add what you can.*
2. *You should attempt to max out the IRA for tax and future purposes. We can make deposits up until April 15 so there is no need to try to do it all in one shot.*
3. *I think the potential for the global fund to grow over the next 18 months is outstanding. European markets leading up to 1992 when the EEC is supposed to come together should rise dramatically. I think we should systematically add to that fund on a monthly basis so we can get the max benefit from those potentially high rates of return.*
4. *If/when the brown car sells, keep the proceeds set aside for my new car fund. Also, try to make periodic additions to it so I can put a bigger down payment on the new car. Leasing is still an option also.*

All of the above are just suggestions. I'm sure you will make sound decisions. I do trust your judgement.

Not much more to report at this time. I love you more than you realize. Can't wait to be with you again.

Always,

Stephen

27 OCTOBER, 1990
1320 HRS.

Dear Diane,

I got two more letters from you today. I also got another letter from Gord and Marie. They are really doing a wonderful job writing to me. I like the station-ery with the yellow roses. It's very sweet.

I'd prefer if you did not send a videotape. But, pictures would be great. I'm still fooling around with the initial roll of film I started shooting. I suppose I'll get done sooner or later. I'm still a little leery about sending it back through the fucked up mail system. I'm sure the system will be over burdened leading up to Christmas.

I'm still doing well. I'm trying to stay in shape by doing at least 100 push ups a day. I think that I have stopped losing weight. I may actually start to pick up a pound or two if I continue to take better care of myself. Also, I am taking my vitamins everyday, believe it or not. ☺

The other day, Kevin Brau asked me when the subject of marriage first came up between us. As I recall, it was the first time we were at EPCOT as we were leaving the Canadian exhibit when you said "it sure would be nice to have a honeymoon in Canada" or words to that effect. I don't remember what I said. Come to think of it, you were the first to initiate a lot of things in our relationship. I guess you just could not resist my cute little body. Frankly, I don't blame you. ☺

FYI, I have puts thoughts of a 300ZX out of my mind for now. I think we should concentrate on building up the biggest "war chest" that we can. I plan to start actively pursuing civilian employment in the summer of 1993. That way I would give myself almost a full year to find the right situation before my ETS.[24] And, if something presents itself sooner, we can leave the green machine sooner. Yeah!

I miss you so much and I think of you very often. Your letters are wonderful. They make me feel like we are still connected. You are right. I don't think we will lose our closeness even if I am here a long time. I think our relationship is rock solid and will withstand whatever comes.

In your last letter you eluded to Liz's foxes. I don't know what that is but it sounds kind of strange. Don't believe the rumors that we will be home by Christmas because I don't. Try to hang on to April 11 as my date of return. If I return any sooner, consider it a blessing. Regarding information, yours is probably better than mine because you get CNN. The Division Commander (two stars) is briefing us again on Nov. 4. Maybe he will be able to shed more light on the subject. However, I'm not counting on it.

Keep hanging in there. I love you with all my might.

Always,
Stephen

---

[24] ETS: End Term Separation, which refers to when your time in a duty station is up.

28 OCTOBER, 1990
1645 HRS.

Dear Diane,

Another day in paradise. I usually don't get the chance to write in the after-noon, but today I decided to make the time. I'm still doing pretty well. I'm really looking forward to receiving the care package that you sent me. I won't promise that I will read The Hobbit Trilogy (it is really not my kind of read-ing). However, I will make the effort for you!

After receipt of this letter a few days may go by before you get another one. We're going out on a GDP exercise for two or three days to conduct a recon of the area that we may have to fight in. I guess it will be nice to get away from the area that we have been in for the past few weeks. Only the officers are going. We take off at 0500 tomorrow morning.

I have a couple of requests. I think this camera is broken. It has been awhile since I used it. When I tried to take pictures today it was completely unre-sponsive. Please send a replacement. Another inexpensive one will do. Sorry...

I don't intend to try to call you. Access to phones is tenuous. Besides, with your schedule I would hate to call and get the answering machine. Just con-tinue to write as you have been doing. Because of your excellent writing, the bond between us is still secure. That knowledge is the only thing that keeps me going.

Are you still keeping a list of the things I miss? A few more items to add: I miss wearing civilian clothes, especially the nice pants that you've bought for me and my nice suits. I also miss being able to sleep in at least one day a week.

I've heard that the U.S. is planning to send at least 100,000 more troops here. I don't know what that means. But if the intent is to kick Saddam's ass then *it's a good thing. The sooner they get here, the sooner we can kick his ass, the sooner we can come home.*

If my stay here is prolonged, I see one or two positive aspects. 1. I'll have lots of leave days built up so we take lots of trips. 2. Bills will be paid off and we will have money to spend on our trips. 3. I will appreciate you more.

I don't know if I've told you this before, but for some reason I've acquired the nickname "Desert Fox." I don't know how I got it. Someone started calling me that one day and I guess it just stuck.

Looking ahead to our 5ᵗʰ anniversary, I think a luxury cruise is probably more feasible than Hong Kong. We have always wanted to take a cruise together. I think that we should go ahead and do it.

How's work? How's the brown car?

I just want to let you know again how proud I am of the job that you are doing keeping things together. You are a wonderful person and I truly consider myself lucky to have you.

Take care and be good.

Love always,
Stephen

p.s. Did my Perspectives piece arrive yet? I hope so.

p.s. I did get the AT&T card and the $50 (the first that you sent).

31 OCTOBER, 1990
0830 HRS.

Dear Diane,

Happy Halloween! Of course by the time this gets to you Halloween will have long since been over. We got back from our little exercise last night. We did a lot of driving around. It was very interesting. I'm glad to know that you are still having fun. Dinner at Michelle's sounds like a good time.

In recent days I've gotten letters from your parents and Ron Buchholz. Ron sent a care package with books and UNO cards. I thought that was nice. Yes, we will have to cruise to Ft. Myers when I get back. I have to write to Zak and Cody. Also, I got a letter from my brother Tony. He is here in the country. He says he has been here about a week. I don't know if we will be able to see each other though. We'll see.

Thanks for sending me the order form for the book-of-the-month club. That was very sweet. I ordered 4 books. As they arrive, just pile them in the closet off my office. I'll tackle them one-by-one when I get back. I'm look forward to that among other things.

Sorry again about the camera. I guess the sand just got to it. I'll do a better job of taking care of the replacement when you send it.

I still have not received the care package that you sent to me around 13 or 14 October. Maybe it's just bogged down in the system. You have to be smart about how you label the box.

I'm glad that someone is very interested in the brown car. Maybe by the time you get this letter it will be gone. That would be great. By the way, how is the Nissan doing? I'm sure that you are taking great care of it. We only owe payments on it for another 15 or 16 months. It will be great when that is paid off.

DEAR DIANE

I know that you are making progress in the financial area. But, I still feel like our lives have been put on hold. I'll be so happy when we can get on with it again. The next three years will be very important for us. We'll have to work hard and save and invest wisely. Pursuing a master's will take time and sacrifice. But, I have to get it before I leave the Army so I can help secure our family's future. However, we will mange to have lots of fun. We'll have to put a higher premium on being together. I know that we can do it.

Not much more to report at this time. Continue to take care of things as you have been doing. Before you know it we will be together again. I love you very much.

Always,
Stephen

four

NOVEMBER 1990

Waiting...

A s days turned into weeks, and weeks into months, we settled into our surroundings even in the face of continued uncertainty. Thanksgiving was right around the corner and the holiday was shaping up to be unlike anything any of us had ever experienced before. We had turkey and dressing, all right, and I was grateful for the attention to this most American of holidays. But celebrating Thanksgiving with your fellow soldiers in tents in the desert is a far cry from celebrating it with family and friends in your own home.

In addition to thinking about my family, I also thought about my friends. During my tour in Germany, I had grown close to a handful of guys, all fellow lieutenants, and I wondered how they were doing. J.D. was no longer on active duty, but I know that his heart was with me. Paul was stuck in some stateside assignment, but I know he wanted to be where the action was in the theater of operations, like any good soldier would. John had deployed with his unit from Germany, so he was in the desert somewhere as well, no doubt kicking some serious butt. And Jim was also in the theater. He actually tracked me down and paid me a visit, which was very cool.

As close as I had grown to those guys in Germany, Operation Desert Shield/Desert Storm was a different order of magnitude, and I formed a bond with a fellow soldier that will be with me for the rest of my life. If Diane was my link to sanity on the home front, Kevin Brau was my link to sanity in the desert.

Kevin was the battalion S-4, which made him my partner in crime. On the surface we were quite different. He is white. I'm black. He is a West Point graduate. I was commissioned from a very small college ROTC program. I was married at the time, he was still a bachelor. Kevin tended to be analytical; I tended to be more impatient. I had no problem dropping the F-bomb; Kevin didn't feel the need to pepper his language with expletives.

Despite our differences, a friendship started to form from our shared responsibility. I have no idea how or why, but soon we started calling each other "Bubba," a nickname that has stuck ever since. On rare occasion we would disrupt the tension of a command and staff meeting by simultaneously breaking out into a rendition of "U Can't Touch This" by MC Hammer. I'm not kidding.

One of my favorite memories with Kevin happened after we were given an order, the logic of which neither of us understood. But afterward, Kevin, because he was an S-4, managed to procure a couple of steaks and a propane stove. We cooked those babies up and chowed down in the back of an M577 personnel carrier, savoring every bite. This unified act of defiance – we could have gotten our asses chewed for something like this – was as delicious as the steaks. It was a moment I will never forget.

Over time our friendship grew into absolute trust. We could laugh together and argue without fear our differences would cause any damage. We commiserated and confided in each other. Simply put, I'm eternally grateful that Kevin was there with me. He helped keep me grounded. Now, when I hear other soldiers and former soldiers talk about their war buddies and what they mean to them, I get it. And, I am proud to say that I love the guy.

Sometime after we had returned from our deployment, I was preparing to transition from the military to the corporate world and I had given my prospective employer Kevin's name as a reference. Kevin told me that the corporate representative asked him if "Steve Bradshaw was a reliable guy," to which Kevin responded, "I would trust this man with my life, because I have."

What can you say to that, except that the sentiment is mutual. It was then, and remains so. In the years since, Kevin and I have not stayed in touch all that well, and I regret that. Physical distance and life's responsibilities have contributed to that. But, it's not a good excuse. Maybe in the future we will do better. Even so, I know the bond between us is still there.

And by the way, I got the job.

1 NOVEMBER, 1990
0840 HRS.

Dear Diane,

Thanks so much for the photos. They really brightened my day. I sure wish I could have been at Sandy and Rich's wedding. It looks like it was very nice. I also like the pictures of you and Paul. You are such a cutie pie. I wish I could give you a big smooch right now.

Today marks the beginning of another month and day 70 of our deployment. I'm still hanging in there, taking it one day at a time. As the days drag on, soldiers become more restless. Rumors are running rampant all over. I try not to put much stock in any of them, especially ones that indicate that we'll be home before Christmas. I just don't see it happening. Supposedly, the official rotation schedule will be announced within the next 2-3 weeks. I'll be interested to hear what that involves.

The other day in the Stars and Stripes some 24th ID soldiers were quoted as expressing their displeasure about just sitting here without knowing one way or the other what's going to happen. The article was entitled "As Desert Temps Cool Soldiers' Temps Heat Up." I'm sure the higher ups don't like that kind of press. But, I'm glad that the true feelings of soldiers are being exposed.

In recent days I've given serious consideration to braces. Yes braces. One of my soldiers had a similar problem with his bottom row of teeth as I have. He says he got his done at the Ft. Benning dental clinic. He wore braces for two years and got them removed right before deploying here. If I get them, I'll only get them on my bottom row and I won't wear them any longer than two years. But, as you have stated before, in the long run it will be worth it. I agree. I'm sure you are surprised.

My mail flow continues to be good. I got a letter from Karen (Tony's wife) yesterday. It was nice. I can't believe that it's been over 4 years since I've seen them. My (our) oldest nephew is probably as big as I am now.

I'm sorry you never got the "baby" letter. It basically was a litany of what I thought about all the options available to us. I left it open ended. You answered my questions in one of your letters, so I guess our minds were on the same wavelength, which is good. I will be happy with adopted children. Now the question is when do we start pursuing the adoption process?

Thanks again for your daily letters. I feel as close to you as I ever have. Maybe closer. Just continue to be strong. We'll be together again soon.

Love always,
Stephen

3 NOVEMBER, 1990
1845 HRS.

Dear Diane,

Thanks for the care package. It arrived two days ago. Sorry I was not able to get back with you sooner. The last two days have been kind of busy for me. I've basically been charged with escorting the press around whenever they show. They have been here the last two days.

The care package was great. You really enclosed some good stuff. Some of the guys were jealous about the size of it. I just told them that my honey loves me very much.

Tomorrow the general shows up. I caught a preview of his text when I was doing business at another battalion today. I don't expect any revelations from it. Just more of the same "I don't know." I have heard that the official rotation plan will be announced within the next two to three weeks. We'll see. Just keep your fingers crossed for good news.

In recent days I have received letters from Joyce (your sister), your parents, my grandmother, Ron Buchholz and John and Laurie Moses. Ron's letter was 5 pages long. He also enclosed some family pictures. He's really a good guy. I like him a lot and will write soon.

John and Laurie are doing great. It seems that Laurie may have the opportunity to work at The White House Communications Agency. Her current Brigade Commander is going there and has offered her the chance to work for him. Because of that, John will probably stay in the Army for awhile longer. There will probably be a long separation for them as Laurie would ETS in October of 1991 and John in September of 1992 (including a 6-month curtailment). If all goes well, they will be in Washington, D.C. together in the winter of 1992. It would be great to have more friends in D.C. to visit.

I'm still doing fine. I think of you often, but I know you are doing well. Being away from you is difficult, but I am dealing with it as best I can. I guess the prospect of being here for at least a year is still a real possibility. Another 9-10 months apart would be a tough pill to swallow. I just hope that the strain on our relationship is not great enough to break the bond that we have.

Sometimes I feel guilty about bringing you into all of this. I know that this is not the kind of life that you envisioned for yourself. I know that succumbing to the "needs of the Army" has been hard for you. I know that your independence has been restricted. Maybe you would have been happier with someone who led a more normal existence – someone a little less ambitious, a little less driven. I can't help it. Despite Saudi '90, the Army will still be my life for at least three more years. When I do leave it will be on my own terms. I just hope that we as a family will be able to survive all of this.

On the lighter side, I think getting a mess dress uniform will be worth the investment. My intent upon return is to make contact through letters with the state Democratic (yes, Democratic) party leaders and the movers and shakers in Atlanta. I plan to present myself as a guy who wants to grow up in the party. If, over my remaining years in service, we're invited to fund raisers and cocktail parties, the uniform (and Saudi '90 experience) will be impressive. The intent is to be viewed and billed as an "up and comer." Before I'm 50 I want to be in a position to give the governorship a serious run. I've got to get started now.

Also in the political view, I caught in the paper that my friend Chris Meredith (you met him briefly in Savannah last November) is running for Congress. The piece was about the money (or more accurately lack of money) in his campaign war chest. I'm sure he'll lose on Election Day since our district is historically democratic, but I know he'll have great insights.

I guess I'll close for now. I do love you very much. Take care and be good.

Always,
Stephen

7 NOVEMBER, 1990
0910 HRS.

Dear Diane,

First of all, don't be alarmed by the mail being taped. I'm doing it just to ensure that the letters stay sealed. I don't believe that any of the mail that you've sent me has been tampered with.

Sorry, I have not written to you in a few days. In addition to professional correspondence, I've also decided to write letters to some others who have sent me mail in the last few days. I've written to Betsy Kohler, Joyce (your sister), Ron Buchholz, your parents, my sister-in-law Karen, my nephews Tony Jr., and Cory and I still owe a letter to Marie and Gord.

I'm glad you got the Desert Fox videotape that was sent. I'm glad that you were able to see me in the videotape. I decided to keep it short and sweet, but I think you know how much I love you.

I seem to be getting Scott in trouble. He told me the other day that because I write to you so much Michelle is starting to give him a hard time about not writing as much. Just tell her that he is really getting into being a platoon leader and that he is staying very busy. This is not to say that I'm not staying busy. I just make the time to write to my little Buchie-boo. ☺ I intend to send Michelle a letter very soon just to say hello and hopefully adequately address her concerns.

How is the job going? It sounds like you are pretty close to finding something that suits you. I hope you do. I want to see you happy in your working envi-ronment. Have you given any consideration to getting a master's in Nursing? Not necessarily to continue in units, but to teach. Emory University in Atlanta has a great medical reputation. With your experience and talent you would no doubt make a great teacher. Just something to think about...

You can also add a few more books to your shopping list for me. Please get all of these in hardcover. I've got the paperbacks. Billy Bathgate by E.L. Doctorow, Out of Bounds by Jim Brown (the former football star), and One L by Scott Turow. I hope that you are enjoying yourself in the bookstores while you are shopping for these. By the way, did Liz ever return my copy of The Burden of Proof? Just checking... What's going on with her and La-Poon-tang these days? Also, whenever you send another care package, please send some more long envelopes and a 1991 calendar (a small one).

Since you are managing to lead the family to financial stability, and since you are handling this whole situation with flying colors, I have made a decision. Regarding your engagement ring and your sapphire ring, I have decided to trade up. My honey deserves a bigger diamond and a bigger cocktail ring. I'm sure that you are going to say that it's unnecessary, but it is something that I very much want to do. So let me do it. After all, you do deserve it.

I'm still doing fine. One day at a time. Still waiting for the official rotation schedule to be announced. I hope the news is good news. I hope that we don't have to fight. I hope that we all make it home safe and sound.

I still miss you more than I can possibly put into words. And I love you more than that.

Always,

Stephen

AKA "The Desert Fox"

10 NOVEMBER, 1990
1545 HRS.

Dear Diane,

Your letter writing has been prolific. I'm very proud of you. I am also getting spoiled as I now expect to get a letter from you every day. In recent days I've received letters from Marie and Gord (they have been just great), Jo Poston, my sister and Nina Turcato. Nowadays it's a real challenge to keep up my letter writing with all of the other shit that I'm doing. But it's the type of challenge that I love. I'm enjoying the mail very much. You're right... you should receive credit for the circle of friends that we have. If it was not for that I would hardly be getting any mail at all, except from you. Just one more reason why I'm glad that you are NOT more like me.

I'm glad that you finally got the baby letter. I'm also glad that you are pursuing getting OB-GYN info. In my heart I would like for us to have at least one baby of our own. A beautiful little girl named Catherine who looked like her mom...☺

Have you bought the computer yet? I've got an idea on where to put the computer. If you arrange the closet off my office a little better, a small desk could go right on that wall that the metal shelf is against. Of course it would mean moving that stuff somewhere else. It's just a thought.

Have you gotten rid of any of your clothes yet? You have so many. I'm sure that Goodwill Industries could use them. Besides, we should get you some new clothes. Maybe maternity clothes somewhere down the road.

I'm glad that my article made it [into the newspaper].[25] Getting my ideas published is step one in establishing myself as an up and comer. Remember, the future is now.

I don't have any special requests for Christmas. If people continue to send letters and pictures that would be just fine. Anything in addition to that would be fine also. I'd like for you to send me a box of Christmas cards so that I can send to people. I think that would be very nice.

Thanks for sending Mary L.'s address. I plan to send her a letter welcoming her to the desert ASAP! I'm glad that you and Mike have become friends. I can't believe I have never met him. It sounds like that was some pool match that you guys had. I'm looking forward to playing again when I get back.

I did receive the second care package. Thanks. In the next one, please enclose some AA batteries. These Army brand don't last very long. I thought your selection of tapes was a little strange. Hopefully, that will improve the next time around.

[25] See Appendix A for the full article that ran in the *Columbus Ledger-Enquirer.*

DEAR DIANE

I'm glad that you caught me on video. Yes, I am known as the Desert Fox. Don't ask me why. Someone started calling me that and I guess it just stuck. No, I do not chew tobacco now. I don't know what it was in my mouth that day. But, it was not that nasty stuff.

We do get newspapers. We get USA Today, Stars and Stripes, the Columbus Ledger and the Atlanta Journal. They usually run about 5-7 days behind, but it's still good to get some news. However, I have not seen any election results yet. I'm very interested.

No, I have not had the chance to lounge in Panther Paradise. I'm staff, which means that I work my ass off to make commanders' lives easier, so says LTC S. But, it's not just me. It's the entire staff. Oh well... Really, it's not as bad as it seems. I make time to rest and do the things I want to do, like write my honey.

Congrats on your purchase of the floor lamp. I know that you wanted one badly. Go ahead and send the DCU. I could use the extra set.

Not much more to report right now. I love you very much. But, I know that you already know that. Take care and be good.

Always,
Stephen

12 NOVEMBER, 1990
2130 HRS.

Dear Diane,

Another night in paradise. I normally don't write letters at night. My mind usually functions better in the morning. But I decided that I would write to you before going to sleep. There are enough things on tap for tomorrow to keep me occupied. It is a beautiful night. The stars are out and shining brightly. We never did get to sit in the gazebo in one of the squares in Savannah and watch the stars. I'm sure that we'll have plenty of chances in the future. There are a great many things that I'm looking forward to doing with you in the future. Once we get through this ordeal, I know that we'll be just fine. Especially after we have 12 babies who all look like you. ☺

I guess you know by now that the U.S. is sending 100,000+ more troops to the region. I'm kinda surprised that 3rd ID is not coming. I guess someone has to keep the peace in Europe. With that I guess you also know that the rotation plan has been sidelined. I know that it was necessary to do so. I'm glad that the additional troops are coming. 1. It gives the U.S. more flexibility to launch an offensive. 2. If an offensive is launched, casualties I feel would be substantially less and spread around. 3. If Saddam sees the light and pulls his forces out then it makes a rotation plan easier and quicker to implement. I guess you also know that the Georgia 48th National Guard Brigade is being activated, which means that Kenneth could find himself over here as well. I know that won't please my mom. I hope that she holds up alright.

Now don't get discouraged. All of these developments may be the impetus that is needed to bring this crisis to a head once and for all. Keep your chin up. There is no need to worry. I still intend to come back home to you so that I can do wild and wonderful things to your body with no clothes on. ☺

I have a few more book requests to keep you busy. Get the new Ronald Reagan book. I've already read a lot of books about the Reagan administration, but he was the President. Also, there is a new book out by Lewis Grizzard called *If I Ever Get Back to Georgia, I'm Gonna Nail My Feet to the Ground.* Considering the circumstances, I think that that's extremely appropriate. I was going to ask you to get the new Donald Trump book but, he doesn't need the money.

I think it's kind of cute that the Gold Fund is yours and the International Fund is mine. We can have a family investment competition to see which one does better. The best part is that it all stays in the family no matter who wins. With regard to the CD, continue to add to it as it matures. But, don't invest for more than 6 months at a time. The ½ % point is not worth losing the flexibility to do what we want with our money. With regard to the IRA, do what you feel is best. I trust your judgement. Just consider this: 20 years from now I can see maybe drawing some of it out to pay for Katherine and Elmo's college education. Also, I think it should stay solely in your name with me as the beneficiary. You will reach 59½ before I will when we can start drawing from it without penalty.

Well, not much more to report at this time. You are always with me. I love you more than anything else in the entire world. The thought of one day being with you again is the only thing that keeps me going. I'll hang in there for however long it takes. And I know you will do the same. Take care and be good.

Always,

Stephen

p.s. You can tell Allstate to shove it up their ass. You can do whatever you want with the money.

2nd p.s. Have a Happy Thanksgiving.

13 NOVEMBER, 1990
1010 HRS.

Dear Diane,

Not much has happened since I wrote to you last night. I just felt like letting you know again how much I love you and miss you. We're gearing up for Thanksgiving. I found out that President Bush will be having Thanksgiving dinner in the 197th Brigade area. He's eating with 2-18 Infantry that is just down the road from us. I think that is amazing. It should be a real dog and pony show. I'm glad he is not coming here, although I would personally like to have a word with old George. Somehow I don't think that that's going to happen.

Right now we are in the middle of a shamal. Going outside is pretty rough right now. I think I'm going to stay in my tent until it stops. Have you shot any pool lately? Do we still have the brown car? Are you taking care of yourself? How is the job hunt going?

I did write to Mary L., welcoming her to this desert paradise. I hope that she responds. How is her husband holding up? What's going on with Liz and Jim? I have not heard from them in awhile.

Not much more to say at this time. Continue to hang in there. Think happy thoughts. Before you know it we'll be back together again. Take care and be good.

Love always,
Stephen

DEAR DIANE

14 NOVEMBER, 1990
1430 HRS.

Dear Diane,

I can't begin to tell you how great it was to talk to you on the phone this morning, if only for a little while. I had almost forgotten how much impact the sound of your voice has on me. Just hearing you made me remember all of your cute little mannerisms and especially how cute you look when you ask for smoochies. Believe me, when I get back I'll give you all the smoochies you want. ☺

Your last letter stated that you were in bed watching Moneyline and Crossfire. I guess hanging out with me all this time has had an effect on you. Sounds like you are turning into a very savvy investor with you daily market watching. I'm very proud of you. I still know that over the long haul that International fund is going to make us a lot of money.

A note of interest: One of the soldiers who reports to SFC[26] Hawk used to be a real estate broker in Atlanta. He's got a lot of insights into the market. I think he may prove to be very helpful. Keep that in mind for future reference.

I saw Scott today. He says that Michelle has been giving him a hard time lately about him deploying. I guess you know that he was on the non-deployable list and asked to have his name removed. In my mind he clearly did the right thing. But, I don't know if Michelle fully understands that. If it had been me, I would have done the same thing. I think you know that. Maybe as she grows a little older she will come to understand. I hope so.

Yes, Georgia taxes are kicking us in the ass. Oh well.

I had a feeling that the whole vibrator thing was kind of a joke. That seemed

[26] SFC: The Army abbreviation for Sergeant First Class.

just a little out of character for you. Believe me, I miss that aspect of our lives also. Once we are back together, it will be sort of like when we first started seeing each other. I remember how we used to make love for hours. I think the fact that it was new had something to do with it. However, I feel also the fact that we simply had great action together had a lot to do with it. You are the most loving person that I have ever known.

We are still hoping for the best. Maybe someone within the Iraqi government will grab their balls and kill Saddam Hussein once and for all. Football season is over half over. Basketball season just started. I missed the U.S. Open tennis tournament. And one guy is responsible. He must pay.

I'll say goodbye for now. I love you more than anything.

Always,

Stephen

15 NOVEMBER, 1990
0930 HRS.

Dear Diane,

After having a little more time to reflect, I'm beginning wonder if talking to you on the phone helped me or made things worse. As I stated previously, it was certainly great to hear your voice. On that there is no doubt. But since that time my emptiness and loneliness have seemingly become more acute. I have not felt any get-up-and-go in the last 24-36 hours. I know that I will get over it in a day or two. But, right now I am missing you a whole lot. It hurts. Or to use your phrase "it's pissing me off."

Right now we are in the middle of a Command Post Exercise (CPX). It is moving kind of slow at the moment. I'm sure things will be hopping around 2 or 3 a.m. Off in the distance I hear artillery shells falling. No need to worry, it's ours. The cannon-cockers are getting a little practice in. We are definitely going to need those guys if bullets start flying.

If the mail holds true to form, you won't get this until after Thanksgiving. I hope that it goes/went well and I hope that you give/gave Anna and Larry my best.

Christmas is just around the corner. I still don't have any specific request. I would love to be home, but I know that is not going to happen. The Division Commander says that he is ordering 18,000 victory Christmas stockings. Whoopie! What I would really like to see are the Christmas stockings that Joyce made for us hanging in our apartment with both of us there to stuff them. Oh well.

It seems like diplomatic activity has been picking up as of late. I think everyone is starting to realize that the U.S. is serious about kicking ass, in light of the massive amount of forces headed this way. Personally, I'll be glad when they get here. Then we can either shit or get off the pot. Right now I think it could go either way.

I'm glad that you are managing to have some fun. A young lady named Mary (the girlfriend of 2LT[27] Tom Herthel) writes that you are a good person and that you have been very nice to her. Of course, I have always known that you were a good person.

I wish I could give you a big hug right now. You give the best huggies. ☺ Just continue to keep yourself busy and think good thoughts. Before you know it we'll be back together again.

Take care and be good.

Love always,
Stephen

[27] 2LT: The Army abbreviation for Second Lieutenant.

Dear Diane,

I'm finally feeling back to normal, or as normal as I can be considering my environment. The loneliness and emptiness is still there but it is not as acute as it was right after I talked to you. I'm fine now. I think I'll be okay for another month or so. I'm still taking it one day at a time.

How are things on the home front? I know that you are still doing fine. I've stated it before, but I'll state it again: I am extremely proud of you. I'm convinced more with each passing day that marrying you was the best decision I have made in my life.

So the brown car is going to remain part of the family. I can live with that. After all of the money that has gone into it, it should be fine. And I will be more confident driving it. It is paid for, which is good. You have a backup vehicle in case the Nissan gets sick. The decision is yours of course. If you get what you are asking, go for it. But, if you decide to keep it, all I ask is that you put a decent stereo system in it. Nothing fancy. You know that my ear is not as discerning as yours. ☺ You can call it my welcome home present. We could also use a nice set of luggage. I know we will be making a lot of little trips when I return, so it will get used. But, aside from that, a nice set of luggage is a nice thing to have.

I hope that you are having a good time tracking down books for me. Maybe you will find something among my request that you will enjoy. I hope you don't mind. My requests are just one more little thing that makes me feel like I am connected to what's going on at home.

Lately I've been giving more thought to the West Point gig. Considering my college GPA, I don't know if I am that competitive. But I have been talking to other guys (West Pointers) who have stated that what they are primarily looking for is well-rounded, smart guys who present a strong, commanding military presence. I think I have all of that. My long range goals have not changed. Personally I don't think that getting to where I want to get will be served by spending three years in New York. I am not giving it serious consideration, I just wanted to let you know that I was thinking about it.

Regarding the Gulf Crisis, I honestly believe that something has to give by March. There is just no way around it. My pledge to be home by our anniversary is still valid. ☺ Just take care of yourself. Work hard. Stay busy. Save money. Think happy thoughts. And be good. I'll be with you soon.

Love always,
Stephen

21 NOVEMBER, 1990
0900 HRS.

Dear Diane,

Today marks day 90 of our deployment. At this point I'm not any clearer on what's going to happen than I was on day one. I've managed to make it this far still in good health, relatively good spirits and managing to retain my sanity. I know that this situation has been equally difficult for you. Maybe more so. But, I know that we will both hang in there for as long as it takes.

Tomorrow is Thanksgiving. I'm glad that you will be able to spend it with good people. I know that you all will be thinking of me just as I will be thinking of you. Despite our separation, which is a pain in the ass, we have much to be thankful for.

How is Michelle these days? I hope that she is doing okay. She seems like a really sweet person. I know that you are a good influence on her. Also, the BICC's (2LT Tom

Herthel) girlfriend Mary speaks very highly of you. You are mentioned a lot in her letters to Tom. My honey is a nice person.

I had a long chat with the Brigade IG[28] yesterday, CPT. McGuire. He was once the S-1 of 2-69. It was very enlightening. He feels that the 197th morale right now is about 7 out of 10. He says it will probably go down to 5 over the holiday season. If the situation stays as it is leading into mid-January he says that we may be facing the potential for some serious problems. I think that he may be right. This stalemate can't go on indefinitely. Something has to give. But, if we are still in a wait and see mode come January 15 with no clear indicators, one way or the other we may be in for some turbulent times. I hope that I'm wrong. Some might say that we are soldiers and as such we should just suck it up. But even soldiers are human beings.

I have another book request. It is entitled Daly Life by Chuck Daly, coach of the Detroit Pistons. While you are at it you can pick me up a copy of Drive by Larry Bird. Both in hardcover. I'll read them when I get home. Thanks baby.

I've asked MAJ. M. the Brigade S-1 to get me a copy of the infamous command list so that I can see exactly how many guys at Ft. Benning are in front of me. If the list is long and it looks like I may have to wait 18-24 months, I'm going to try to do the following: In whatever comp time they give us when we return I will knock out my CAS 3[29] correspondence. Then request to go as soon as possible. Upon my return, instead of going back to 2-69, I'm thinking about taking a job on main post with regular hours so that I can pursue a master's degree more easily and cool my jets until a command is available. Don't tell anyone this, but I don't want to command for any longer than 12 months. After that I'll look for another job on the main post that facilitates me actively pursuing civilian employment. If you can't tell, my patience with the green machine is wearing thin.

---

[28] IG: The abbreviation for Inspector General.
[29] CAS 3: A correspondence course required before attending the Command and General Staff College, a military school that prepares officers for field-grade responsibilities.

DEAR DIANE

Well, not much more to report at this time. You know that I love you more than anything. Even more than brussell sprouts. ☺ Take care and be good.

Always,
Stephen

22 NOVEMBER, 1990
0830 HRS.

Dear Diane,

Happy Thanksgiving baby! I sure wish that we could be together, but I know that we can't. Believe it or not my spirits are pretty good today. I know that you will enjoy yourself with Anna and Larry and that makes me happy.

I got the care package yesterday. WOW! What a care package! You are just so sweet. I promise I will take much better care of the electronics equipment this time. I'll take plenty of pictures and I will make recordings on the cassette mini tapes and get them to you in time for Christmas. I also got two letters and a little message from you and Lizella today. Very timely… I'm glad that you are enclosing my GQ magazines in the supplemental package. Don't forget the Atlanta magazines.

I hope that your trip to Atlanta went well. I'm sure if you linked up with Jo Poston you had a good time. How are Sandy and Rich? How is Sandy's pregnancy going? I hope that everything is going well.

I could probably use a little more cash. I am not in dire straights now. But, by the time this gets to you and you get back to me, I will probably need a little. No more than $50. Also, a few more razor blades would be great. Just a little insurance.

Today, I also got a letter from Mary L. It was very nice to hear from her. It sounds as if she is doing pretty well. She seems to have adjusted to desert life okay. I still don't know if we will actually be able to see each other. But, I know where she is and I'll try to see if we can link up. By the way, have you shot any pool with Mike lately?

Not much more to report at this time. Thanks again for the continued support. You have been just wonderful, wonderful, wonderful. But, I did not expect anything less. Take care and be good.

Love always,
Stephen

24 NOVEMBER, 1990
1600 HRS.

Dear Diane,

Another day in paradise. Not much has happened since the last time that I wrote to you. I'm still hanging in there, taking things one day at a time.

I did have somewhat of a surprise today. I got a postcard from Joyce Peter's boyfriend in Canada. It didn't say a whole lot. He just wished me luck and said that maybe one day we could get together for a cold beer. I thought that was rather nice. You will have to tell Joyce the next time that you talk to her.

I'm still taking care of myself. I hope you are doing the same. How is Michelle doing? On Thanksgiving I saw Scott. He had some pictures from the wives Halloween party. You looked real cute as the hobo. Where did you get that hat? It looked good on you.

I found out yesterday that Margaret Thatcher has quit as Prime Minister. That is quite a shock. Oh well, nothing lasts forever.

Not much more to say right now. You will hear from me again soon. I love you very much.

Always,
Stephen

DEAR DIANE

Dear Diane,

Another day in paradise. We continue to wait, seemingly waiting for the other shoe to drop. As it stands now we are still no closer to a solution. I've stopped trying to speculate, even though I am tempted to. I still believe that whatever is going to happen will take place between now and March 1. Maybe even between now and February 1. No need to worry. Nothing will happen to me.

I got a letter from Sandy today on Ritz Carlton stationery. She seems to be doing well and getting used to the idea of being a mommy. She says it is probably going to be a boy. She even enclosed a picture of the ultrasound. Very interesting. She also sent a few pictures from the wedding of you. You really did look good that day. I don't believe I have seen that particular dress before. Is it new? Of course it would have to be blue. ☺

FYI – I have started a subscription to Inc. magazine. It was 83% off the cover price. They should begin to arrive in 6-8 weeks. You can send those to me as they come. By the way, have any of the books that I have ordered started to arrive yet? Just curious. Speaking of books, I have two more requests for you. Murder at the Kennedy Center by Margaret Truman and The Content of Our Character: A New Vision of Race in America by Shelby Steele. These two are pretty recent, so you might be able to catch them in a Waldenbooks. Also, if you are tired of looking for some of the older books in books stores you can try to order them through Waldenbooks. Sometimes they can dig 'em up. Sometimes they can't. Anyway, thanks for doing this for me.

If you are still looking for a computer it might be best to wait until after Christmas for the big sales. I'm sure you are already thinking that.

Someone took a Polaroid of me, so I decided to enclose it. I'll try to get you some 35mm pictures and at least one mini cassette by Christmas. Speaking of Christmas, I don't want you to be sad or to feel alone. You are lucky in that you have a lot of people who love you and care about you. You can be grateful for that. I am grateful that I have you. Just knowing that you are there keeping the home fires burning is a Christmas present enough for me. I also hope that you get lots of visitors after the first of the year.

Remember, I miss you more than I can possibly put into words, and I love you more than that. Take care and be good.

Always,
Stephen

28 NOVEMBER, 1990
0700 HRS.

Dear Diane,

You are spoiling me. I just got another care package from you today and it was filled with great stuff. Thanks so much. Your tape selections this time were great. I probably won't need another care package for awhile. I have started to make a mini cassette tape for you. It will be coming along in awhile. And some pictures. My goal is to get it to you before Christmas. We'll see...

I found the piece about your friend Tom Smith (The Stat Man) very interesting. So you know some famous people. That's good. Maybe I will get the chance to meet him someday.

Wisconsin for Christmas next year sounds good. But, I am not looking forward to braving the weather.

I have been giving some more thought to the West Point gig. I think I am going to request more info and see where it leads me. The only way that I would *accept is if they let me major in what I want (Public Policy or International Relations) and if they let me go to the school of my choice (Emory University in Atlanta). Aside from that, it would not fit into my plans. When I think about it, two years of just going to school, and three years of teaching in the pristine environment of West Point, NY, does not sound so bad. It would give us the opportunity to be together and spend time with the babies. I still plan to get a master's in Columbus also. I want to keep all of my options open, just in case they don't want me.*

The U.N. should be voting soon on whether to use force in Iraq. I hear that President Bush wants a January 1 ultimatum attached. It is looking more and more like we may be getting our own chance at glory after all. We'll see. Don't worry. I will be fine.

Not much more to report at this time. I love you. I love you. I love you. With all of my heart.

Always,
Stephen

30 NOVEMBER, 1990
0045 HRS.

Dear Diane,

After being deployed for 100 days it looks like things are going to get hot. We have received intelligence reports that Saddam is moving massive amounts of troops into Kuwait. It looks as if he is preparing to attack. Prime time is between now and December 2. The moon will be full and there will be 100% illumination. At this point I cling to one last shred of hope that someone within his government will rise up and dispose of him. But, I feel that the chances of that are very slim. War is more likely imminent. This may very well be the last correspondence that you get from me.

I will try not to make this too long and drawn out. But, if for some reason I am unable to return to you, please know this: Knowing you and loving you has made my life complete. I never knew that I was capable of feeling as strongly about someone as I do about you. You have changed my life for the better. You have caused me to see things I might have never seen. And feel things I might never have felt. Your love has made me whole. For that I am grateful. I will carry that love with me throughout eternity.

If I don't come back, please do not mourn for me too long. You are a very attractive person and any man would be lucky to have you. My only regret is not having children. I wish I could leave you with something as evidence of our union. I know that in the course of time memory will fade. There is nothing that we can do about it now.

I don't know what else I can say except goodbye, take care, I love you.

Always,
Stephen

five

DECEMBER 1990

Waiting...

C hristmas in the desert was approaching. With each passing day, the idea of a potential holiday homecoming faded a little bit more. Truth be told, I had not been excited about the holiday season since I was a young boy. The hoopla surrounding it all tended to grate on me, and to a large extent it still does. The shopping and decorating and parties and family drama and obligations of all kinds seem to induce more stress in people than genuine holiday spirit. Even so, the miracle that is Christmas has never been lost on me, which I owe to my religious upbringing.

But as Christmas 1990 approached I kind of missed all of the craziness. Doing without it all was just not normal and it made me a little sad. My melancholy was underscored by a profound sense of longing for my wife, friends and family.

My brother Tony is 7 years older than me, and the age difference made being close a little prohibitive. I was around 11 years old when he left home to join the Army, and that was pretty much that. We have not really spent that much time together in the years that have passed since then.

My brother Ken is about 2 ½ years younger than me, and as kids we did a lot together. But, as we moved into our adolescent years we followed our own paths and drifted apart. In recent years, as we have moved through our 40's, we have started to become a little closer. Whenever we get together for a beer these days we usually end up laughing our heads off about some silliness that we experienced as kids.

My sister Alethia is 5 years younger than me, and we have never been all that close. However, I recall being fascinated by her when she was a baby. Not long after she came home from the hospital I reached into her crib to pick her up for a closer look. Needless to say, I was not supposed to be doing that unsupervised at age 5. When I heard my mom coming down the hall I panicked and abruptly dropped her back into the crib so I could get out of there. In turn she let loose a scream that got everyone's attention and me into big trouble. It's probably a good thing she does not remember that. Otherwise, we might even be more distant.

Irrespective of the varying degrees of closeness, there is still nothing like family. And we all do care about each other.

Then there are my parents, Raymond and Mary Bradshaw. By the time I deployed to the Gulf they had long since been legally separated. And a tremendous amount of acrimony surrounded all of that. I'm sure that they loved each other once. There were indeed times when I was growing up when they seemed happy together. But, those moments as I recall were few and far between. Simply stated, they struck me as two people not very well suited for one another. Moreover, I am convinced that the long separations, due to my father's service in the U.S. Navy, had to be a contributing factor in their struggles. That is no one's fault. That's just the way it is. As I have gotten older my thoughts and feelings about both of my parents have morphed and evolved. Maturity has induced a certain amount of clarity that has produced certain judgements that I will keep to myself.

After going through the normal ups and downs in my own marriage I have come to a theory about marriage: No one really knows what goes on within the confines of a marriage except for those two people. Outside observers might think they know. But they don't. Not really. That is why I am reluctant to ever comment on anyone else's marriage, from those of my friends to couples that I see on TV or in tabloid newspapers. And that's why comments on my parents' relationship will end now.

The important thing is that I know they both loved me. And I know that my deployment caused them to worry albeit in different ways. While I was deployed, facing an uncertain future, my brother Tony was as well. And my brother Ken's National Guard Unit was at the National Training Center in California, preparing to join us in the desert had that become necessary. Alethia was still at home, but all three of my mother's boys faced potential danger. And I cannot begin to imagine what she must have been going through.

When a loved one is deployed, spouses worry. Friends and family members worry. But a parent's worry – particularly a mother's worry – is another kind of hell. My mom has always been deeply religious. Her father was a Baptist minister, and the church was a significant part of our lives growing up. Whatever moral compass I have is in large measure attributable to all those Sunday mornings I spent in the pews. I owe both of my parents for that. Surely my mother's faith in God helped to sustain her during this very trying time. Still, I know she worried, and that knowledge hurt my heart.

My father, also the child of a minister, worried too, and I'm sure he relied on his faith as well to get him through. Additionally, as a former military man, he was equipped with a different frame of reference and coping mechanisms that helped him deal with it all in a different way. Therefore, I did not worry about him as much.

But I was very concerned for my mom. The image of her and my sister at the chain link fence, saying goodbye, had stuck with me since, and Christmas approaching made the memory even more haunting. I prayed often, asking Our Heavenly Father to give my mother peace and comfort.

The movie *Saving Private Ryan* was released in 1998. I had the honor of being in Normandy, France, for the 45th anniversary of the allied invasion in 1989, and I think that experience made the movie that much more impactful for me. There's a scene in the movie that moved me in the most profound way, and still does. The scene, which uses no dialogue, opens with a woman in the kitchen of a farm house doing dishes when she notices a car kicking up a dust plume down the road to her front door. As the car draws closer it becomes apparent that it is an official military vehicle. As the woman watches the oncoming car, she slowly makes her way to the front door. We, the viewers, presume that the woman is the mother of Private James Ryan and his brothers and we know that Private Ryan's brothers have all been killed in action. In a prior scene the actor playing General George C. Marshall has shared with members of his staff President Lincoln's Letter to Mrs. Bixby. Mrs. Bixby apparently had several sons who all served and died in the Civil War. And this was the catalyst for initiating the mission to save Private Ryan from the fate that his brothers had met.

The woman reaches her front porch just as the staff car stops and two very serious looking men emerge from the vehicle. Whatever these men have to say just can't be good. And before a single word is exchanged she collapses in a heap right there.

The first time I saw that scene I could not stop myself from crying, because it made me think of my own mother and what she must have gone through. By this time I had long since returned from the Middle East. But that scene jolted me and took me back to a time when my mom must have been worried sick. It made me sad all over again. It made me think of all mothers: those who worry for children in danger and those who grieve for children lost.

1 DECEMBER, 1990
0845 HRS.

Dear Diane,

As of this writing the other shoe is yet to drop. I hope that my last letter was not too melodramatic and I hope that I didn't upset you too much. What I wrote was what I felt at the time. We are still faced with a situation where we could be attacked at any time. I'm still praying for peace. We'll see.

The care package with the GQ mags arrived a few days ago. Thanks! You are doing a great job. Your tape selections are good.

In recent days I received letters from Katherine Butler (Liz's mom), Jeanne Reese, your parents, a package from Marie and Gord, and a letter from a cousin who lives outside of Chicago whom I have not seen in many years. I also got two letters from my honey today. Thanks honey. ☺

I'm glad that the car finally sold. $2,150 was a good price. I guess I will start to give some consideration to the kind of new car that I would like to get upon my return. But, I suppose I don't need to devote too much thought to that at this time. I know that you are happy that the brown car is gone. So am I. I know you never liked it that much.

Your father said that my Perspectives article ran in the newspaper in Shawano.[30] He says that it got a lot of favorable responses. I'm glad. I'm sure he will send you a copy.

Jeanne Reese's letter was three typewritten pages. It was very nice. She says we will have to do another party at Rita's house upon my return. Sounds good to me.

---

[30] See Appendix A for the article that ran in the *Shawano Evening Leader, The Columbus Ledger-Enquirer,* and the *Savannah Morning News.*

There is a lot more that I could say right now but I want to get to some other letters, so I will cut this a little short. I'm sure I will write to you again tomorrow.

As of now I'm fine. My health is good and my spirits are good. My focus is clear. Don't worry. I will be fine. Take care and be good.

Love always,
Stephen

4 DECEMBER, 1990
0730 HRS.

Dear Diane,

How are things on the home front? I hope that everything is fine. Today is just another day in paradise. Things seem to have calmed down back to normal. But things got to be a little tense the last couple of days. The day before yesterday we got a report that Iraq had launched SCUD-B missiles and that they were on a flight path to either Israel or Jordan. Needless to say we were scrambling. A lot of people were ordered to go to MOPP-4.[31] Later we discovered that it was just a test and that the missiles had landed within the borders of Iraq. Believe it or not, I really did not panic. However, I am glad that it did not start the war. Now it seems as if peace talks have a chance. I sure hope so, I'm still praying for the best.

I'm glad to hear that my article made the Shawano paper and I'm glad that it got a favorable response. I don't feel that I'm ready to rival Rich as a journalist; however, I am glad that my views had a chance to be heard.

In recent days I have received a letter and care package from Wendi, and letter from Tony and believe it or not, a letter from my father. It surprised the

---

[31] MOPP: Army abbreviation for Mission Oriented Protective Posture (protective gear).

shit out of me.

December 1 was supposed to be the day that all of our bills were paid off. I hope that happened. I know that you have been doing a good job. I'm very proud. Speaking of finances, I have figured up what I will make this year (total) and what I will make next year if the current pay raise plan takes effect.

1990		1991
$30,468	*Basic Pay*	$31,716
5,940	*Housing Allowance*	6,180
1,476	*Subsistence Allowance*	1,548
$37,884		$39,444

For some reason it just does not seem like I make that much. Where does it go? Actually, I know. Our jewelry has been somewhat of an extravagance. Your car is very nice. ☺ *Our furniture purchases have been top quality (which I feel we deserve). Our artwork is valuable. We did take a lot of good trips while in Europe. Plus we live fairly well. I know that we have much to show for our hard work. It just doesn't seem like it. I know that you are doing a good job with the money. And I know that you will save lots now that we are out of debt. I just can't help being nervous about money. I guess growing up seemingly always having to worry about it had an effect on me. Oh well. Just one of my many foibles that you have to live with.*

Well, not much more to report at this time. I love you so much. I think the fact that you played back my answering machine message 20 times is very cute. But then again so are you.

Always,

Stephen

p.s. Make sure when you go to frame the copy of the article that your parents sent that the newspaper's heading and date are included. Thanks!

DEAR DIANE

Dear Diane,

Another day in paradise. Things have pretty much reverted back to business as usual. I'm still doing fine. My health is good and my spirits are relatively high. The remainder of the month looks like it will be very busy. We are going to be drawing M1A1 tanks like we had in Germany. They will be sending me back to the post in Damman for some training. Since I have already been on these tanks it should be just refresher training for me.

Where we will be located is not too far from where Mary L. is located, at least compared to where I am now. If it is at all possible, I am going to try to see her. Her last letter said that she would love to see me if I was ever in her neck of the woods. I would like to see her too. By the way, have you shot pool with Mike lately?

I have looked through the new car book that you sent me. I think I have decided upon an Acura Integra. It looks nice and it seems to be reliable. And it will have more room than the Nissan. The price parameter for the 1990 models is $11,950–6,675. I will probably be able to get all I need for about $14,000–15,000. I know there is an Acura dealer in Columbus. Start inquiring to get an initial feel. I would like to be able to put about $5000 down. We'll see. A Mercedes 190 would sure be nice. But I don't think we can afford the $31,000 price tag. ☺

I have been thinking about babies again lately. When do you think you should have the procedure? Where? Do you think you want to wait until I return? Can we afford to wait that long? I don't want your health to be in jeopardy. What do the docs say? Realistically, I think we will only be able to have one baby together. I'm sure if we want more we will have to adopt. I don't see why we should wait any longer. Continue to think about it.

I think I may soon have a political contact. CPT Y.N. Myers, our BMO[32], has an uncle who is the assistant to the Secretary of State of Georgia. I have known Y.N. since 1986 when we were AOB[33] lieutenant together at Ft. Knox. Anyway, he gave me his uncle's address at the state capitol. I am going to write him an introductory letter and see where it gets me. All I need is a foot in the door. Remember, the future is now.

I am glad to hear that you are still dieting. Continue to hang in there. I remember the success you were having with the program at Ft. Knox and how great you were looking. I am confident that you can do even better. But remember, I still love you no matter what.

Not much more to report at this time. Continue to hope and pray for the best. Take care and be good.

Love always,
Stephen

12 DECEMBER, 1990
1900 HRS.

Dear Diane,

I am sorry for not having written in the last few days, but things have been sort of busy. Right now the battalion is going through transition to the M1A1 tank. Also, a few nights ago we had a dining-in. You remember what I went through planning formal affairs in Germany. Just imagine what I went through trying to put one together out here. It was quite an experience. All in all things turned out all right, but I just couldn't sit back and enjoy myself. The life of the S-1.

---

[32] BMO: Abbreviation for Battalion Maintenance Officer, the person who oversees and manages the maintenance for all of the battalion's equipment.
[33] AOB: Abbreviation for Armor Officer's Basic Course.

DEAR DIANE

I'm glad that they finally offered you the GS-11[34] job. You deserve it. Whether you take it or not is totally up to you. I just want you to be happy in your work situation.

Guess what? I was able to see Mary L. yesterday. She is located not very far from where we are going through transition training. It was great to see her. She seems to be doing very well. I really do like her a lot and I think that we will really be good friends. If things go well I will be able to see her again tomorrow. She told me that you and Mike have seen each other some. That's good. She is already looking forward to things that the four of us can do together once we get back.

I'm glad that you decided to straighten out the filing cabinet and my desk. I am sure I will appreciate it. I think I will appreciate you more also. I love you so much. Sometimes I'm amazed by how deep my feelings for you run. I never thought I would be capable of this much feeling. I guess you just brought that out of me.

In recent days I have received care packages from Joyce P., Rita Olsen and Ann Brown. I also got another letter from Marie and Gord. Apparently mom and dad showed them a copy of my article. They were impressed. By the way, I hope that you have gotten a nice frame for it. ☺ That was hopefully the first of many thoughts of mine that will be published.

How are you now? I hope your spirits are still high. I am sure that seeing Liz over New Year's will be good for you. Just be careful on the highway. How is dieting? I won't push it. Just keep on working at it.

I dropped a Christmas card in the mail to you with pictures of me. It should arrive within a day or two of this letter. I hope you like the pictures. I have dropped a few pounds but I am still in pretty good shape. I do lots of push ups daily. When I return I am going on a massive weight/strength gain program.

---

[34] GS-11 is a type of classification for a federal government job.

DECEMBER 1990

As I approach my 28th birthday I am becoming more conscious of such things. My goal is to equal or surpass the shape I was in as a 23 year old AOB lieutenant. You remember how good I looked when we met in Chicago that one time. That is what I want. That is what I will attain. I have to. It is a matter of pride.

Not much more to report again at this time. I am still hoping for the best. Maybe something good will happen soon and all of this will be over. I sure hope so. Take care and be good. I love you.

Always,
Stephen

15 DECEMBER, 1990
1430 HRS.

Dear Diane,

I was able to see Mary again. We had a really nice visit. She seems to be doing well. She looks good and her spirits seem to be high. We took several pictures together. I will send them as soon as they get developed. Seeing her really did lift my spirits. I am becoming very fond of her. She wants the four of us to do things together once we return. I think that would be very nice. I hope that Mike, Rex and Charmer are doing okay too.

15 January is the big day. It is good to have something to focus on. I still have no idea which way this will go. I'm trying to get myself in the mindset that says we will be rolling north come 16 January. I can tell you that my resilience is starting to wear thin. I know that I will hang in there for the duration but it is not getting any easier. I miss you so much sometimes that it hurts. I would give anything just to be able to touch you again. Mornings are still the hardest part of the day for me. Waking up to the realization that I am still here is tough. But, it does not last for very long. Usually the bullshit starts shortly after I fall out of the fart sack.

I got a letter from Anna today that told of your Thanksgiving visit. Have you done something different to your hair? Anna remarked in her letter about how great your hair looked. I know my honey is a cutie pie.

I am glad that you got all of the bills paid off and you were able to send $1,500 to the IRA. I hope it does help with the taxes. I know that you will do a good job with the new car fund. It should be much easier to save now. However, I don't think that you should stop depositing to our funds completely. Smaller periodic deposits would probably still be good. How much and how often is entirely up to you.

I hope that you will be okay even with Liz and Jim now gone. I hope that you don't miss them too terribly much.

Not much more to report at this time, I want you. I need you. I love you, with all my heart.

Always,
Stephen

16 DECEMBER, 1990
1730 HRS.

Dear Diane,

I got a package from Joyce and Bob today with a cassette tape in it. It was very nice and they were very funny. It made my day.

Being back at the port in Damman for transition training was like old home week. I ran into at least 7 soldiers that were in A Company 1-69 when I was

XO. It was really good to see all of those guys. I also ran into Greg H. Honestly, I never really cared for him that much back in Kitzengen. But, it was a familiar face.

By the way, if you talk to J.D. tell him I ran into Ho-Jo and had a picture taken with him. If he does not catch on right away use this quote: "First Sergeant, no disrespect but I think that I got fucked on my Class 1[35] this morning." He should catch on then.

I hope you got the pictures that I sent by now. I won't enclose any in this letter, but I will send more periodically. Then you can decide which ones you want to keep and which you want to send to people.

I am still taking it one day at a time and hoping for the best. I would give anything just to see you again. I hope that won't be too much longer. I miss you more than I can possibly put into words. And I love you more than that.

Always,
Stephen

p.s. I also got a letter from John Moses today. His unit is en route. He seems to be a little apprehensive. I don't blame him. Anyway, he and Laurie send their best to you.

---

[35] There are several classifications of supply items that soldiers use on a daily basis; Class 1 refers to food. This notation is an inside joke referring to Private Howard not getting breakfast on a particular morning in Germany.

DEAR DIANE

Dear Diane,

I just got another care package from you today. Thanks so much. You must be reading my mind regarding the tape selections. I guess you just know me well, which is good. The box got here pretty fast. The post mark was dated 10 December. I think that boxes are traveling much faster than letter mail. My only request is that instead of Underwood products, send Spreadables instead. Thanks.

Have some of the books that I ordered started to arrive yet? Again, just put them in the closet. I'll tackle them one by one when I return. I hope you don't mind paying for them.

FYI – I took a $50 casual pay on 15 December, just so you are not surprised. I know you are still doing well with the money. Remember, save, save, save. It seems as if we are becoming a regular DINK (double income, no kids) couple. We will soon have two new cars, an expensive apartment with expensive furnishings (by the way, Mary commented on how nice she thought our place looked), nice jewelry and enough money left over to do what we want.

The goal is still to be able to buy a nice house in Atlanta area. I checked in a magazine recently about real estate prices in that area. Starter homes run about $65–85k. Trade-up homes about $115–150k. And executive homes from $225–400k. I figure if we work and save for the rest of my time in uniform, land good paying jobs in Atlanta and get a little help from your parents we will probably be able to comfortably afford something in the $150–175k range. Of course comfortably is the key. We'll see. I am just very excited about the prospect of our future together.

Oh well. Not much more to say right now. You are my one and only honey. I love you so much. I have not mentioned sex in awhile. It is because I am trying not to think about it. I think you know how I feel about that part of our relationship. I want lots of it when I get back. ☺ Take care and be good.

Always,
Stephen

22 DECEMBER, 1990
1415 HRS.

Dear Diane,

At last, the long letter that I promised you. First let me say that it certainly was good talking to you the other night. You really sounded great. It made me feel good to know that you are taking care of yourself. Afterwards I did not feel sad at all. I was just very grateful and thankful that I have you as my honey. I was also able to talk to my mom and Sandy and Rich on the same day. My mom sounded good and was happy to talk to me. She also stated that you have been very sweet, which is something that I have come to expect. Needless to say Sandy was very surprised. It sounds like being pregnant is agreeing with her. I can't wait to see what this baby turns out like.

Speaking of babies, I am very happy that you are starting to get excited about the thought of having our own. I am excited too. Although I can't do much about it from here. I think a child of ours would be beautiful. It would have a funny looking nose, but it would have a great personality and be very smart. I hope that your fertility procedures continue to go well. Also, I think that we would make great parents.

I am glad that the wives' Christmas party went well. I might have known that your crab things would be a hit. You and Michelle deserve pats on the back. I can hardly wait until I am able to eat your cooking again.

I think I told you that I got a letter and package from Dick and Kristi. I thought that was very nice and I was very surprised. I responded immediately. I have also gotten packages from Karen (your sister) and your parents in recent days. I really have a lot of stuff now. I should be set for awhile. However, you can continue to send magazines. I really look forward to getting them.

On 20 December we had a tree lighting ceremony. As always, social gatherings are a pain in the ass for me. But, it turned out well. We had about 15 American civilians who work for the Aramco Oil Company come out and celebrate with us. They brought lots of stuff, and one even dressed up as Santa Claus. Unfortunately, I did not get any pictures of the event.

Regarding the books that I have ordered, I think that it is a good idea that you have put a six-month freeze on it. There will be plenty of time for me to start it up again once I return. Also, I have another one that you can look for. First Lady From Plains by Rosalyn Carter. I just finished reading the paperback and found it to be very interesting. I would like for you to look for the hardcover. Thanks.

Now on the financial side of things, I'm glad that you have decided to stop adding to the Gold fund. I just looked through the December issue of Money magazine and their projections are that gold will do well in 1991. $2,500 is not that much money, so I don't think we need to pull any out. We can afford to let it ride and just see what happens. On the other hand, the Global fund should go up, according to those same projections. As far as I am concerned, the more you add to that one the better off we'll be. I am also glad that you sent $1,500 to the IRA. Years from now having that money in the IRA is going to save us a lot of grief. Your decision on the insurance was a good one. I signed the form and sent it out today. It should arrive within days of this letter. The CD should be maturing around your birthday. Upon maturing, you should buy another one for six months. If you don't have the money to increase it, just buy another for $10,000 plus the interest earned on the first one. I regard the CD as our backstop just in case everything else goes to shit.

STEPHEN R. BRADSHAW
Captain, Armor
United States Army

22 AUG 90

Dear Diane,

This is probably the hardest letter I have ever had to write. There is so much that I wish to say to you. There are probably a lot of things I wish I had not said at times. But the past cannot be changed.

I don't know how events will play out. I am a little unnerved. But I fully intend to return home to you hopefully unscarred mentally or physically.

I know I have not always been the husband that you want me to be. I know there have been times when I have seemed thoughtless, uncaring and down-right mean. But I want you to know that I have never intentionally hurt you. Nor would I want to. You don't deserve it.

Sometimes you have been a gigantic pain in the ass. ☺ But all-in-all you have been a wonderful wife. You have been all that I've wanted and

This is a portion of the first letter I wrote to Diane after I was deployed. The check mark is a notation that I made when I started this project.

Diane and I at our third wedding reception at the American Legion Hall in Bonduel, Wisconsin. This is one of my favorite pictures of us.

Kevin Brau and me. Kevin was my best friend and my sanity check during the course of our deployment, for which I am forever grateful.

I'm not sure what I was doing here. I think I was trying to look menacing. Obviously, I failed miserably.

James Lafayette Haynsworth IV, a.k.a. James La Poon Tang and me. I gave him that nickname as a play on his middle name. Jim's visit that day was a very welcome surprise.

One of our luxurious toilet facilities.

Getting some news from the "doom and gloom daily."

Mary Laedtke and me at her location. Her husband Mike Brennecke and Michelle pictured on the next page) looked after Diane while we were deployed. I will always be grateful for that.

Michelle Suhr (Prosek) and Diane at a Halloween pajama party. Don't ask.

Me and Jeff Williams. Jeff introduced me to the idea of being an instructor at the Officer Candidate School. Jeff was an all-around good guy.

At the airport in Bangor, Maine, with my most adoring fan.

Me and one of the local residents.

A more recent photo of Diane and me. Another one of my favorites, taken by our friend, Kathy Davison.

By the way, how is the new car fund doing? Also, I decided to accept the Chevy Chase Gold Card. The $6,000 limit is very convenient. I only ordered one for me. I figured that you have a $6,000–7,000 limit on your Citibank Gold Card. I don't think we need any more than that. The temptation for me to spend would be too great.

Speaking of spending, you are going to have to help me control my urge to buy lots of new suits when I get back. I really don't need another one at all right now. Continue to make purchases for yourself and the apartment as you see fit. You deserve to have some fun. I cannot overstate how proud I am of the way you are handling things. We have a great partnership. I am very lucky.

I am still doing well. Hoping for the best. I hope that you are maintaining your spirits. I know that we will be together again soon. The thought of spending the next 71½ years with you is the only thing that keeps me going. ☺ Thanks for your love. You know that you have mine.

Always,
Stephen

p.s. In addition to Katherine, what do you think of Ivey as a possible girl's name? Then we always have Audra Rae to fall back on. If it's a boy his name will be Elmo Dwayne Bradshaw. On this there will be no negotiating. ☺

23 DECEMBER, 1990
0700 HRS.

Dear Diane,

This will be a short note. I got a nice Christmas card and pictures from Linda and Joel in Columbus, OH. Robin is really cute. I think she still has a crush on me, which I think is very sweet. She will obviously grow up to have very good taste in men. ☺ *Also, it looks as if Joanna will have some serious competition for my affection. But, I think there is enough of me to go around for everybody. Of course, my honey will always be my number one.*

I will get through Christmas and New Year's all right. Staying busy will help me keep my mind off of home and hearth.

Try not to worry about me. I am managing to take care of myself. And in the event of war, I will survive. I have to.

Not much more to report at this time. More pictures will follow. Take care and be good.

Love always,
Stephen

24 DECEMBER, 1990
1100 HRS.

Dear Diane,

It is Christmas Eve, but somehow it does not feel like it. My environment stays the same. The bullshit continues. I am just not in the Ho! Ho! Ho! frame of mind. I am thankful for my health and sanity. I am also thankful for all the friends and family members that we have who have been extremely supportive since I have been away. I am still cognizant of what Christmas really means. And it certainly is ironic that I am in this part of the world right now. Most of all, I am thankful that I have you, the best honey in the world.

Maintaining my motivation gets just a little bit harder with each passing day. Don't worry. I will survive. But, it is not getting any easier. On 15 January I guess we will know what our future will bring. At this point I think it would take a miracle to avert conflict. I know that the pace will be fast and furious and very messy. We will just have to wait and see what happens.

I will turn to a more pleasant topic now. To tell you the truth I am trying very hard not to think about sex (although I do smile when I think about it). I do miss the physical aspect of our relationship very much. But, I will hang tough until I get home. I really don't have a choice.

You probably won't get this until after you return from New Year's Eve with the Haynsworths. I just hope you have a good time.

I don't have much more to report at this time. Please continue to take care of yourself. I don't have any idea how much longer we will be forced to be apart. But, I know that we will both endure for however long it takes. I miss you more than I can possibly put into words. And I love you even more than that.

Always,
Stephen

25 DECEMBER, 1990
1255 HRS.

Dear Diane,

Well, it's Christmas Day. But, I am certainly not in the Christmas spirit. This morning I did my laundry and straightened up my living area. Within the coming weeks I will be sending certain things home. I am trying to lighten my load in anticipation of when we are called to move. You can continue to send things like magazines and food stuffs. I will consume them. Just don't send anything of value. It will end up getting sent back to you or left here in place.

Right now a shamal is going on outside. It is the worst that I have seen so far. I am planning to stay inside this tent as much as possible.

DEAR DIANE

I have caught a cold. I am not feeling the greatest right now. Maybe that is the reason that some of the zing has been taken out of my Ho! Ho! Ho! Don't worry. I'm sure it will be over in a day or two.

As to this business of war, I am completely convinced that it is coming. Within 30 days we will know for sure. When it comes it is going to be fast, furious and very violent. I just hope that I survive.

By the way, did you ever hear anything from Maria Mowbray? Just curious. What about Marie Bayer?

Just continue to do what you have been doing. Are you liking the pictures that I have sent to you? I hope so. More will be on the way.

Not much more to report at this time. Take care and be good. I love you.

Always,
Stephen

25 DECEMBER, 1990
1720 HRS.

Dear Diane,

Well, the sun is setting on a Christmas that I'm sure I won't be forgetting for some time to come, if ever. The shamal has lasted the whole day. Walking around outside has been an adventure today.

I have been taking Tylenol today, so my cold seems to be doing a little better. The meal that our cooks put out today was excellent, as always. I ate well. Don't worry about my weight. I think the picture should show that I am maintaining.

My spirits are good, despite the fact that my motivation has slipped a little. For a unit that may be engaged in combat in 30 days or less, we (some people) seem to be placing an emphasis on stupid bullshit, in my opinion. I won't even elaborate. I just hope that that changes as D-day draws near.

I love you! That's my statement.

Stephen

26 DECEMBER, 1990
1200 HRS.

Dear Diane,

It is the day after Christmas and I survived. The shamal ended last night. My cold is a little better and I'm just in a better frame of mind than yesterday.

I hope that Christmas for you was tolerable. I know that you worked, which was probably a good idea. By the time you get this you will have returned from your New Year's Eve trip. I am sure that you had a good time.

For the past week, the Saudi Gazette should have been called the Gloom and Doom Daily. Reading that stuff probably contributed to my overall sullenness. But, there was an article yesterday that basically stated that Saddam would pull out of Kuwait and that he is already laying the groundwork for the PR spin that he is going to put on it. That would be okay by me. The prospect of going to war with this battalion is starting to weigh on me. I just don't have a warm and fuzzy feeling about it. In a way I am sorry that I discovered that article. I was really starting to get in a combat mindset. Now that has been fucked up!

Although I am basically staying on my normal even keel, I have probably experienced more emotional swings since I have been here than at any other time in my life. I will hold on no matter what. Seeing you again is all that matters. Do you still have that list of things that I miss? I've got something to add. I miss wearing my leather jacket, especially now.

I don't know if I have mentioned this before, but it might be a good idea to buy some new luggage for all of the nice little trips that we will take upon my return.

Let me say again how proud I am of you. You have handled yourself like a Trojan Warrior. When I get back I am going to give you a nice present. Me with a bow on my head. ☺ Take care and be good.

Love always,
Stephen

27 DECEMBER, 1990
1520 HRS.

Dear Diane,

It certainly was good talking to you on the phone this morning. Hearing your voice always puts me in a better frame of mind. It sounds like dinner at La Toque with Jo will be a lot of fun. I wish I could be there.

Keep your eyes open for auto bargains. That deal on the Acura Integra sounds pretty good.

I got a letter from your parents today which had a copy of the piece I wrote. I still think that it is amazing.

I still think that we should maintain not less than $10,000 in the CD. I know that we won't make the great interest rates. We should maximize what we *put into the Global fund. But, I just don't want to give up the safety that a CD provides. My aversion to risk is probably greater than yours. I just won't feel safe with anything less than $10,000 in a very safe place. Besides, there are no guarantees with the fund. I think between us we earn enough to add to the fund on a periodic basis. Enough said.*

I am trying to get myself in a "go to war" mindset. It is not easy. But, I am convinced that it is coming and that it won't be pleasant. I guess we will know soon enough. I've got a feeling that between now and January 15 time will fly by. Don't worry. I still plan to come back to you in one piece.

I think it is amazing that Ed and Ruta are really going to come see you. I really wish that I could be there. I think it would be really amazing to see them in something other than a Wisconsin farm setting. If a miracle happens, I will be there. But, don't hold your breath expecting it. Anyway, I know that you guys will have a blast together.

I have enclosed a copy (unedited) of a letter that I sent to my potential contact in the political realm. I know that it is pretty straight forward. But, soon I will be 28. If I ever hope to be in a position to realize my aspirations I have got to start right now. Anyway, I have already mailed the edited letter. I am interested to see what kind of response I get. Just please file this copy. Thanks!

Not much more at this time. Please continue to take care of yourself. We will be together again soon.

Love always,
Stephen

DEAR DIANE

29 DECEMBER, 1990
1700 HRS.

Dear Diane,

I had a dream about you last night. In the dream you had no clothes on. We were having wild action!

I thought that after all this time doing without would become easier. It hasn't. I miss a lot of things about not being at home and action is right there at the top, as you know. But, I won't dwell on it.

I hope that you are still maintaining the list of things that I miss. I have got something to add. I miss wearing my trench coat. It really has a lot of style. Also, I think I am going to buy myself a hat or two once I return.

I thought about trying to call you at Jo Poston's house today as a surprise. But, the timing would have been bad. It would have been 3 a.m. your time if I had called when I had the opportunity. Neither one of you would have appreciated being called at that hour, I don't think.

Anyway, I hope that you were careful on the highway (by wearing your safety belt and not driving so fast). I would not want my honey to get smashed by a big truck or something.

My cold is almost gone and I am in better spirits. 15 January will get here very fast. We'll know something one way or the other. I figure that by 31 January we will either be engaged in heavy combat or we will be preparing to come home. We'll see.

I am still convinced at this point that going to war is more likely. But, I am hoping for a miracle. It would be really wild if I was home in time to greet Ed and Ruta. Of course I would not want to time it too close. I figure that when I get home we will have to stay in bed for at least a week. What I would really like is to have action on top of my desk. ☺ Think about it.

Not much more to report right now. I love you more than anything in the world.

Always,

Stephen

30 DECEMBER, 1990
1215 HRS.

Dear Diane,

Another day in paradise. Today marks T–17 days. That is how long it is before we reach the 15 Jan. deadline that the U.N. has imposed on Iraq. I am sure that the time between now and then will go fast. But, I won't dwell on it.

So, how is your pool game? I understand that Mike beat you the last time that you played. Did you let him win? How did you do at Jim Collins in Savannah? I'm sure you felt good being back there. It seems like 90% of our "dates" were playing pool at Jim's. I especially liked the nights when we were the only ones in the place. We also made a pretty good team. At our peak I know we had to be in the upper 50% of pool shooters in Savannah. Maybe the upper 33%. Although, I would not hazard going much further than that. Who knows? All I know is that we had lots of good times.

When I spoke to Sandy she said that Rich would be interviewing for a job in New York. That is something. If he gets it I will be torn. On the one hand it would be great to have friends to visit in the Big Apple. But, on the other hand, with them not being in Atlanta it just won't be the same. Oh well. Sandy also said that someone that we know from Germany would be in New York also. Who might that be?

There is something to consider for our financial future. If we have the cash by the end of 1991, we should consider buying stock in one or two very strong companies based in Georgia. We should, of course, start small and build a respectable portfolio over time. I am talking about companies like Coca-Cola, Georgia Power, Georgia Pacific etc. In the long run, I think it might be a good idea. What do you think?

I am sure that you will fill me in on your adventures in Savannah and Charleston. I will be looking forward to hearing about them.

Not much more at this time. Take care and be good.

Love,

Stephen

31 DECEMBER, 1990
0700 HRS.

Dear Diane,

Happy New Year!!!! Well almost anyway. Of course, by the time this gets to you the celebration will long since have subsided. I hope that your time visiting was enjoyable.

As I sit here on the threshold of a brand new year I can't help but wonder where we will be this time next year. Who knows? I would like to be able to say that I am 100% sure that I won't be here. But, I won't say that.

As you have probably gathered by now, I spend a fair amount of time thinking about money. I can't help it. I just can't shake what I grew up in. I probably never will. I just wanted you to know, as I have stated before, that I am very proud of the way that you have handled things. But, I will bore you with some more ideas. I have been trying to figure out ways to get into real estate. But, I have not figured it out yet.

I know we will be out of the Army in 2-3 years. Maybe less if the right opportunity comes along. Anyway, I think everything in Atlanta, including real estate, will be on a glide path up leading to 1996. We will see what happens.

Also, if you feel like we want to maximize our money in the Global fund it might be a good idea to transfer $1,000 from the Gold fund. Think about it. There... that wasn't so bad. It's time to move on to other topics.

If they give us some comp time when I get home I would like to spend it just relaxing at home. We can use my built-up leave to do our hopping around at a later time. It should not be a problem. I have 32.5 days right now. The one thing that I would like to do during the comp time is to spend 3 or 4 days doing Atlanta together. This means spending... yes, spending lots of money. We should stay in a nice hotel. Eat good food. Drive around. Shop. Just be together. I would like a new suit (whether I need one or not). I think that we would have lots of fun together as we usually do.

I just got a postcard from Wendi and Barry in Hawaii. Those two are something else. I also got a card from Greg and Dianna Coday. It surprised me. But it was good to hear from them. I think Dianna is enjoying being a mom.

The more I think about it, the more I like the name Ivey for a girl. What do you think of Ivey Caroline Bradshaw? I think that has a nice ring to it. The prospect of maybe being a dad in a year or so really has me very excited. I hope that you are too. I want a little girl that looks just like you.

Not much more to report at this time. I love you more than anything. Even brussell sprouts.

Always,
Stephen

six

JANUARY 1991

Anticipation

U nited Nation Security Council Resolution 678 was passed on November 29, 1990. This resolution gave Iraq a withdrawal deadline of January 15, 1991. Further, it authorized the use of "all necessary means to uphold and implement UN Resolution 660."

Resolution 660, which was passed in early August, condemned Iraq's invasion of Kuwait and demanded withdrawal of all Iraqi forces. Since August, months of negotiations and posturing had taken place. Diplomatic means had now essentially been exhausted and the time for decisive action had come.

By this time, a coalition of forces from 34 countries was assembled in opposition to Iraq. American forces in the region numbered well over 500,000 troops. All of us, including myself, were ready to do our duty.

As the deadline for Iraq's compliance approached, I wondered how long it would be after January 15 before things got ugly. I wondered if Saddam Hussein had any idea what he was up against: the best-trained and equipped fighting force that that had ever been assembled in the history of warfare. I wondered if he thought this was all just a big show, that the coalition really would not attack and that half a million American soldiers had come to the desert for the hell of it. The smartest thing Hussein could have done at this point would have been simply to withdraw his forces and keep them massed on the Kuwaiti border. By doing so, he would have satisfied the UN resolutions, kept his Army intact and continued to remain a threat to Kuwait and the rest of the region.

This maneuver would have left us with a serious conundrum. What would we have done? Would we have attacked anyway? Would we have kept our forces in place as a deterrent (which was highly unfeasible because of the cost and logistics involved)? Or would we have withdrawn, only to have Hussein reinvade Kuwait whenever he felt like it and start this cycle all over again? This would have been a significant problem. Fortunately, Hussein demonstrated he was not that smart.

And although I did not realize it at the time, our prospective action against Iraq did not have overwhelming support in the Congress of the United States. The authorizing vote for the use of military force to drive Iraq from Kuwait was taken on January 12, 1991. In the House of Representatives, there was a decent margin of support for the action in a vote of 250-183. But, the vote in the Senate was much closer: 52-47. I'm not sure what the members in both chambers who voted "no" were thinking at the time, especially in the face of all that had transpired to that point.

I also wondered what was going through the mind of our Commander-in-Chief. President George H.W. Bush struck me as a good man. He seemed to be conscientious, have a good heart and actually care about those whom he had placed in harm's way. Even so, I have lived long enough to know that in our highly competitive political system, no one ascends to that level of power and authority by being "Mr. Nice Guy." I do not believe that any man can occupy that office and put Americans in harm's way in a casual manner. The weight of such a decision is just too great. I believed and still believe that our president had done everything possible to prevent war. And if war was inevitable, he had armed us with the right strategy and tactics to get the job done.

Saddam Hussein had made a colossal miscalculation. He had committed a terrible atrocity. Now it was time to pay.

Dear Diane,

For the first time in over 4 months I have actually seen and felt rain. All of a sudden it started to rain this evening. It was not very hard and did not last very long. But, it was unmistakable. So how is the weather there? I hope that it is tolerable.

The new year arrived for me unceremoniously. At the stroke of midnight I was riding in a CUT–V[36] on a bumpy dirt road trying to get a soldier out of here on emergency leave. I was able to see Mary L. again, which made it all worthwhile. I really do like her a lot. She is a sweet person. She said that she got your Christmas card and would write to you. She also said that she would give you an objective appraisal of how I'm doing.

I guess you know by now that I tried to call you on New Year's Eve. I am sorry that I missed you. But I was able to say hi to Dr. and Mrs. Butler. They are such nice people. Also, I talked briefly with Anna and Larry. Joanna initially answered the phone. I could hardly believe that it was her. It is amazing how fast children grow up. I'm sure that our 12 will be no exception.

I am very proud of the progress that you have made dieting. I am sure that you looked marvelous. Mrs. Butler remarked on how great you look. I can't wait to see you (with no clothes on).

I got a great family picture of the Kohlers. Little Alice certainly has the cheeks. I hope that you had an enjoyable time in Savannah. I'm sure you did.

Two packages from me should be coming your way sometime soon. Instructions are enclosed.

[36] CUT-V: A type of Army vehicle designed for driving over rough terrain.

DEAR DIANE

My emotions have been on a roller coaster for some time now. I just don't know what is going to happen. And I hate not knowing. My patience with this whole ordeal is wearing thin. I am not at the breaking point though. You know me. I will stick it out however long it takes..

FYI – I'm still known as the Desert Fox. Don't ask me why. It just stuck.

Take care and be good.

Love always,
Stephen

3 JANUARY, 1991

Dear Diane,

I feel like I am in the lull before the storm. 15 January is fast approaching. Yet there doesn't seem to be a flurry of activity going on around here. Yet, we're supposed to be "going to war." The bullshit missions persist. I know that everyday leading up to January 15 will be filled with its own distinct pitfalls. Getting through one day at a time with my sanity still in check is my overriding priority. Believe it or not, things will be much easier to deal with once the action starts. Then there will be something to focus on. But for now the waiting is agony. And it's only going to get worse.

To top things off, today has been another shitty day weather wise. More shamals. It sucks! Oh well.

I want so much to be able to see you and talk to you. I spend a lot of time looking at pictures of you, thinking about how we started out. We definitely had some rough spots early on. But, once we made the commitment to each other we never looked back. I have not regretted a single day since.

This exercise has provided me with the opportunity for introspection more than at any other time in my life. I ask myself sometimes if commanding a company is really worth it. All it means is more aggravation and bullshit. I suppose my attitude would be better if the leadership of this battalion was better. S. blows hot and cold. He talks a good game, but I still don't know what he is really made of. R. is a moron. It has gotten to the point where I just hate to see his face. I'm hoping I just don't go off on him one day. MAJ T. is a doofus. In actuality, he is probably the nicest of the three. But he is just incompetent and continually gets squashed by the other two. For my money, I would rather have LTC Coon, MAJ Baker and MAJ Walker. I just don't have a good feeling about going into combat with our current crew of field grades. That is a sad commentary.

In the last letter I got from you, you said that you would not mind me staying in depending on my assignment. Well fuck that! I know this is not what I want anymore. I won't leave the Army before it is financially advantageous for us. But, once we are back, I am giving very serious consideration to seeking a job somewhere on main post or ITC and concentrate on pursuing my master's and leaving the Army as fast as I possibly can. I know that I won't be doing this 5, 10, 20 years from now. So why should I spend all of my effort now? Why?

I am sorry that the tone of this letter has not been any better. It's just the sign of the times. Don't worry. I'm fine. I just need an outlet. Fortunately, I have you.

Thanks for being my wife. Take care and be good.

Love always,
Stephen

P.S. Once all of this is over, I think you will be ready for a promotion to three stars.

DEAR DIANE

5 JANUARY, 1991
1300 HRS.

Dear Diane,

Another gloomy day in the KSA.[37] We must have entered the Saudi rainy season, such that it is. It has been overcast with intermittent rain. It almost reminds me of Germany. But, it's not nearly green enough.

The countdown continues. 15 January can't get here soon enough for me. I am tired of waiting. It sucks. At least by then we will know (or should know). The Saudi paper seems to be indicating a possible softening on Iraq's part. I just don't know. I don't want to get my hopes up. Of course, by the time this gets to you, the 15th will have passed.

I really don't have access to birthday cards. I just want you to know that I have not forgotten it. When January 17 rolls around I will be thinking of you and wishing you the best.

I'm glad that little Sandy is coming to visit. I do like her. Please say hello for me.

I think it would be really wild if Ed and Ruta actually showed up in Columbus, GA, for a visit. I know that you all will have a great time together. I wish that I could be there. But, I know that the chance of that is virtually zero. I refuse to give up hope for April, however.

I can't believe we have been married for almost 4 years. I am looking forward to the next 71 years with you. Even when I get to be an old geezer I will still want lots of action. I'm just giving you fair warning. ☺

It was good to hear your voice again yesterday. You sound really great. I'm

---

[37] KSA: Abbreviation for Kuwaiti Support Area.

sure you look great too. At least that is what everyone says. I can't wait to see you (with no clothes on).

I just sent you two boxes yesterday that you should get sometime soon. I still think that you are doing a wonderful job holding down the fort. I'm very proud of you.

I know that we will have lots of fun together when I return. It will be fun going on little trips. It will be fun just staying at home. It will be fun trying to make a baby.

Not much more to report at this time. Take care and be good.

Love always,
Stephen

8 JANUARY, 1991
1200 HRS.

Dear Diane,

The countdown continues. I guess Baker[38] and Aziz[39] will meet tomorrow. I'm not expecting anything positive to come out of it. I think both sides are too entrenched in their positions to back down. My hopes for a peaceful resolution are all but gone. I just don't see it. Battle plans are being formulated as I write this, although I'm not privy to them just yet. It's just as well. As 15 January draws near I'm filled with trepidation and calm at the same time. I honestly believe that I will return home from this ordeal in tact. I just don't believe that it is my destiny to die in this barren wasteland thousands of miles from home. But, I know that there will be those who don't make it back. And it makes me sad to think about it. By the time this gets to you the battle may already be raging. I think that I am in the right mindset to do what has to be done.

[38] Baker: The US Secretary of State, James Baker.
[39] Aziz: The Iraqi Foreign Minister, Tariq Aziz.

Naturally, I am concerned about the welfare of the entire battalion. I have become friends with some of the guys – especially Kevin Brau – but it is still not 1-69 in the glory days. I am concerned about both of my brothers. I think the loss of any one of us would have a devastating impact on my mother. I am also concerned about Mary. I really like her a lot. I hope that she is able to return home unscathed.

I have spent the morning packing my stuff. I have been forced to get rid of a lot of stuff, some of which I have sent back to you. I have been saving my letters since day one. I decided to count them today. It came to 170 with a large majority of them from my honey. You have been just wonderful in that regard. I hope that you have been satisfied with the amount of mail that you have got from me. I wrote everyone's address down in my address book so that I can send everyone who wrote a personal thank you letter (on my high-speed stationary) upon my return.

I talked to my mom yesterday. She sounded good and said that she was very glad to see you over the holidays. I think that she has really grown very fond of you. She also said that my article ran in the Savannah paper. She also said that you all had a little dedication to me down at Jim's. That's great. I am really looking forward to the day when we can shoot pool together on Jim's table like we did so many times in the old days. We fell in love on Jim's table.

What I feel for you is almost indescribable. I never thought I could feel so strongly about someone else. You are my best friend. You are my honey bunny. You are the future mother of my six children. ☺ Well, maybe not six. I think I would be very happy if we had just one beautiful baby together.

I got a really sweet letter from Joyce Peter the other day. You already know how fond I am of her. And I have liked virtually everyone that you have introduced me to. I am both surprised and touched that so many of them took the time to write to me.

There are many good times and much celebrating to be done once I return. I would like to be able to see everyone and thank them in person for their support. But, before I do that I want to take some time to be with the best wife a man could ever hope for, so that I can tell her how much I love and appreciate her. Hold on to that thought, and before you know it, I'll be there.

Always,

Stephen

16 JANUARY, 1991
1530 HRS.

Dear Diane,

It is 16 January and I'm still kicking. The U.N. deadline passed without incident, so far. I know that it's just a matter of time. Everyone's mindset is now just to get it on. People are tired of waiting. I know that we are going to war. I still don't want to believe it. I never wanted to believe it. But in my mind I always knew it. I think I have stated that in my letters from the beginning. I don't think that it will be much longer. We'll be at war by February 1.

Yesterday we moved from our assembly area to a marshalling area only a little forward. Within a week our heavy equipment will be moved to our tactical assembly area to the north. Way north. My guess is shortly thereafter the Air Force will start bombing the shit out of Iraq and Kuwait. When that stops, then we will be on the move. I hope that the first bomb drops on that son-of-a-bitch responsible for me being here.

Again, I'm not worried about me. As I have stated before, I don't believe that it is my destiny to end up dying in this barren wasteland. I just hope that the fighting ends soon and that we can return home soon. Believe it or not, I'm still clinging to April 10-11 as my date to be home. I am hoping for a joyous birthday-anniversary celebration. The thought of being with you again is all that keeps me going.

So, your birthday is tomorrow. I hope that it's good for you. I think it's good that little Sandy is coming to see you. It should be a fun time for you. Obviously, I wish that I could be there to share the time with you. But, events have dictated otherwise. I know that we have many celebrations to look forward to in the future.

Right now I feel that my life, our lives, are on hold. I don't feel as if I am moving forward. Everything is at a standstill. Yet, I know that I am continuing to move forward.

This experience will shape me or change me in some way that I don't know of yet. I don't think it will be for the worst. Hopefully, I'll come away with a better sense of who I am. I will appreciate things more. Hopefully, I will be a better man.

As you know by now, many thoughts have run through my mind since this whole thing began. I am happy with most of the choices that I have made in my life. Some have been bad decisions. But not many. After lots of soul searching I am still very comfortable with my ambitions. As I look to the horizon from this vantage point, I feel that all are attainable. And maybe even more. It may sound corny, arrogant or otherwise, but I truly believe that greatness is my destiny. Stick with me and it could be yours also. ☺

My letters to you now will be sporadic as the situation dictates. It does not mean that I'm not thinking about you. Please continue to write. The value of your letters will increase tremendously in the coming days.

Not much more to report at this time. Please remember that I miss you more than I can possibly put into words. And I love you even more than that.

21 JANUARY, 1991

Dear Diane,

As you know by now, the war has started. So far the 197th has not been committed to action. But I know that it is coming. It is just a matter of time. It seems like the Air Force is doing a pretty good job of destroying some of his more lethal weapons. The threat of chemicals and artillery still bothers me though. In tank versus tank action I think we will be okay. I just want this whole affair to be over quickly. Believe it or not, I'm still holding out for an April 10-11 return day. My hope is that we will have achieved objectives in 4-6 weeks. Then the powers that be can start to implement some type of rotation plan that can get the troops who have been here the longest out of here.

Maybe the mail has been screwed up lately, but I have not received a letter from you in over a week. Letters from others are trickling in one at a time. I hope that it's something in the system. I would hate to think that people were slacking off at the time I need to hear from home the most.

So how was your birthday? Even at 36 I still think you are a sex biscuit. How was little Sandy's visit? I hope that you guys had a good time together. I think that the hope of being home in time for Ed and Ruta's visit is zero. I hate the fact that I won't be there. I know that Ed being out of Wisconsin again will be an historic event.

The longer I am here, the more leave days I am building up. I should have 35 days by the end of January. Hopefully, the new car fund is continuing to grow also. I know that you are doing a good job with the family finances. We have the future to think about.

Please don't worry about me. I will be fine. Even though the war is going on as I write this, it still seems like something very remote to me. We hear the reports on the radio. It is something akin to listening to a sporting event. I just want it to be over. I just want to be able to hold you again.

I miss you more than I can possibly put into words. And I love you even more than that.

Always,

Stephen

22 JANUARY, 1991
0730 HRS.

Dear Diane,

Last night I got "read on" to "the plan." As you might expect, I can't disclose anything about it to anyone. I will say that it is a good plan and we'll just have to see what happens. I am still hoping for a return date of 10-11 April. But don't be too disappointed if that becomes unfeasible. There are a lot of variables in combat. If this son-of-a-bitch decides to fight to the last man things could get a little nasty. If he comes to his senses and realizes that he can't win in the face of superior military force, then our jobs will be much easier. In any event, we won't be sitting on the sidelines much longer.

This has been a test of endurance. As I look into the faces of the soldiers around me, I see a combination of emotions: excitement and fear, anticipation and trepidation. And I'm sure that they see many of the same things when they look at me. I don't have all the answers. I don't really have any answers. Survival is my objective.

Pretty soon I won't have the time to sit around and think deep thoughts. Once our movement starts, things will be fast and furious. What will keep me going is the thought of seeing you again. I know that day will come, but I don't know when. Just hold on.

On the lighter side, this year's Super Bowl should be very interesting. By the time this gets to you it will be over. But my prediction is Buffalo 24, New York 17.

Again, please continue to write. I still have not received a letter from you in many days as of this writing. I hope that there is nothing wrong.

I am fine both physically and mentally. I still take my vitamins everyday. ☺ I am looking forward to getting home so that I can concentrate on getting in good shape again.

Things are difficult for us now. But, as I have stated before, this could be the event of our lifetime. Years from now when we are financially independent and Ivey and Elmo are in school and we have lots of time together, we will look back on this whole episode and think, "That wasn't so bad."

Just hold on to that thought. And before you know it, I will be there.

Love always,
Stephen

p.s. Will you get my baby picture framed?

23 JANUARY, 1991
0800 HRS.

Dear Diane,

I just got a letter from you dated 3 January. I guess the mail has slowed down considerably. But, I was glad as always to hear from you.

I hope that you are right about 1991 being a better year. It sure has started with a bang. This war is going to be an interesting experience. We will not *just roll over the Iraqi Army. We will win. No doubt about it. But there will be a price. I just hope it is not too high. I wish that the Air Force would just bomb him into submission. But, I know that air power alone has never been decisive in any previous war. I also wish that someone would just take Saddam Hussein out. But, that does not look likely either. I am just not relishing the thought of a ground war.*

If he sees that he is simply facing a superior force he may throw in his cards to keep from being totally decimated. At least I hope so. If he decides to fight to the last man, then it could be a long affair. I want this to end soon so that I can come home on time. But, as each day passes, the thought of an April 10-11 return date grows a little fainter. Right now I am about 85% positive that I'll get home by that time.

I just recently went over the 5-month mark, which is the longest we have ever been apart. It is difficult, but I am hanging in there. I know that you are doing the same. Just try not to be too disappointed if I don't make it back before, say, June 1.

I am glad that you decided to put another $1,000 in the Global Fund. What is our total in that fund now? I am thinking it should be about $5,000. Once again, I commend you for taking care of family finances.

How is the exercise program going? I am sure that you are doing fine. I know that you will be beautiful when I return. Again, don't worry about me. I will continue to write as much as I can for as long as I can. Keep your letters coming. I need to hear from you now more than ever.

Take care and be good.

Love always,
Stephen

JANUARY 1991

Dear Diane,

As long as I have the chance, I will continue to write to you. I know that at some point in the near future the opportunity will disappear.

Nothing is changing immediately. One day is pretty much like another. The anticipation and the pressure are starting to get to some people. S. told us that another battalion commander within the division had been relieved. He could not handle the stress anymore. I guess he just drove himself too hard until he just lost it. Also, within the battalion we had another incident. I have told you in the past what a shithead F. the XO is. Anyway, apparently he asked the NCOIC[40] of the Support Platoon to do something that the sergeant thought was stupid. He (the SFC) said no. The two of them went back and forth for awhile until finally the NCO told F. to get out of his face before he got the shit slapped out of him. The NCO will probably get a general court martial. Oh well.

I am still doing fine. But between F. and J.T., I am a little worried about the fate of this battalion. I am still praying that by some means we will avoid being engaged.

Maybe the Iraqi people will take Saddam out before we have to go get him. I sure hope so.

So where is James La Poon? Are you maintaining any contact with Liz? He will be getting here just in time for action.

Future political considerations notwithstanding, I can live without combat, a chest full of medals, war stories or anything of the kind. I just want to come home.

---

[40] NCOIC: The Army abbreviation for Non-Commissioned Officer In Charge.

If things do not go according to plan, which they never do, this operation could take awhile. Even if we are able to attain out military objectives in 2-3 weeks, restoring stability is a process that would take much, much longer. I would hope that they would pull the units who sustained the fight off line and let some follow on forces take that job. But it may not work out that way. Just don't be too disappointed if I am unable to return home before mid-summer.

Don't worry. We will be fine. 20 years from now we will look back on this whole episode and think, "That wasn't so bad." At least I hope so.

Take care and be good.

Love always,
Stephen

25 JANUARY, 1991
1300 HRS.

Dear Diane,

Another day out of action, which means another day out of potential danger, which suits me just fine. Your letters are starting to trickle in again. The one that I got yesterday was dated 4 January 1991, so it took about 3 weeks. They are also telling us that once we join the fight there could be an additional mail delay of 5-10 days. But, don't stop writing. Once the action stops, if I have got a pile of letters from you waiting for me, that would be just fine.

So how is the book hunt going? I have got another one to add. It's called Army Blue by Lucian K. Truscott IV. I have seen it before in bookstores, so you should be able to find it. You would probably like to read it.

The weather seems to be getting a little better, which is good. I just hope the war is over is over before it gets too hot again. I would hate the idea of being in a chemical suit in 100-degree weather.

Are Ed and Ruta still planning to come? I am really sorry that I am going to miss those guys. My sister wrote that she and my mom were planning to visit you. Did that happen?

I am still hoping for a speedy resolution to this war. But, as I have stated before, things may not work out that way. All I know is that I am in it for the duration, however long that is. You have done a tremendous job holding things together so far. I know that you will hold on for however long it takes.

The more I consider the idea of having a baby with you, the more excited I get. We will have a beautiful child. You will be a wonderful mother. And I will be a wonderful father.

$32,000 a year now, huh! That is almost exactly what I will be making in base pay this year. $64,000 between the two of us is not too bad. It will be really great when we can make $64,000 a year each. ☺ When I think about it, I guess we are kind of yuppies, even though I hate that word. We do well. The 90's will be our decade. Our goal should be to work toward having a net worth of $500,000 by the time 2000 rolls in, including the house that we hope to get someday. I think that it is within the realm of possibility. And, if we fall a little short, so what? If we are over, that's even better.

Even in the face of impending combat, I am looking forward to the future. It is all that keeps me going. I love you. I love you. I love you.

Always,
Stephen

DEAR DIANE

27 JANUARY, 1991
1015 HRS.

Dear Diane,

This may be the last letter of mine that gets out of the country for awhile. Within in the next few days we will be moving to our tactical assembly area near the Saudi/Iraq border. A war that has seemed unreal until now will be very real very soon. I won't say exactly where we are going, but we will be within enemy artillery range. Things will get to be very intense from here on out.

At this point, I don't know what else to say. After all this time I think you know how I feel about you. I still fully expect to make it back to you in one piece. But, there are a lot of variables in war. That is why, to my way of thinking, a quick resolution is the best for all parties concerned. I really hope one of those Air Force bombs kills that crazy son-of-a-bitch so we can get the fuck out of here. I have never been completely comfortable in this environment. The sooner I'm back in the USA, the better.

Please pass along my heartfelt thanks to everyone who has written to me and showed their support over the past 5+ months. At some point it is my hope that I will be able to thank them all in person.

As for the efforts of my honey, I can't begin to thank you enough. I know that you will be there waiting for me when I return. That is the only thing that will keep me going throughout this ordeal.

I won't prolong this letter with fluff because there is no need to. I will simply end by saying that I love you very much.

Always,
Stephen

seven

FEBRUARY 1991

The Battle is Joined

I donned a military uniform for the first time in the late summer of 1977. I was a freshman at Savannah High School and had enrolled in the Junior Reserve Officers Training Corps – JROTC – program. At the time I may have weighed all of 120 pounds soaking wet. So my uniform fitting was a little challenging. Still, I thought I looked pretty good. I was 14 years old.

Three years later, I was awarded the Chatham Artillery Saber as the Cadet Colonel and Commander of the JROTC Brigade. A few years after that, I was a distinguished military graduate from my college ROTC program. That was followed by the Armor Officer's Basic Course, Airborne School, a three-year tour in Germany, holding positions as a Platoon Leader, Battalion Liaison Officer, Company Executive Officer and Battalion S-1. I returned to the United States to attend the Armor Officer's Advanced Course and then held positions as an Assistant Battalion S-3 and Battalion S-1 again.

The previous 13 years of theory, study, training and experience had all led up to this moment: I was about to go to war.

By that point in February, the air war had been going on for about two weeks, and by all accounts it was going very well. We had achieved air superiority in short order. J.J. Isherwood was an Air Force Captain assigned to our task force as the air liaison officer (ALO). He was a fighter pilot, and in our command and staff meetings his animated descriptions of what his fly-boy brothers were doing was both informative and very entertaining.

Up until then, in my ignorance I did not think much of Air Force guys. In fact, I thought they were kind of soft – lots of Army guys did. A lot of it was jealousy about our perceptions of them – their housing was better, their food was better and they were all kind of candy asses. Well, I was wrong. The damage that they were inflicting on Iraq's war-making capability was devastating. And I am so glad they were on our side. I would not have wanted to be an Iraqi soldier on the ground dealing with the constant reign of terror they inflicted from the sky. That continuous bombing must have been quite unpleasant.

Even so, those Iraqi soldiers were not going to be dislodged from their positions by air power alone. That meant decisive action by us, the ground soldiers, and a ground war seemed more inevitable with each passing day. As this reality set in, I became more serious, more focused and more in touch with the idea of my own mortality.

Over the holidays Diane had made a trip to Savannah to visit my family, which I thought was very sweet. While there, she made a stop at the place where we had many of our dates, Jim Collins Bar. It was a Savannah institution and a world-class dive near the corner of Whitaker and State streets.

The place was the antithesis of pretentiousness. It was small, dank and dusty, with one bathroom shared by both men and women and an old juke-box that had not been updated since who knows when. An autographed picture of blues singer Leon Redbone hung on the wall, commemorating the time a few years back when he'd stopped in and played a song or two. In the center of the room was a small pool table that cost 50 cents per game.

The proprietor was Jim Collins, who was a character to say the least. On weekday evenings, passersby would have a hard time determining if the place was actually open because, from the street, it appeared that all the lights were out. Despite the darkness, it was always open. We would usually find Jim in a corner behind the bar, reading the Savannah paper by the light of a small lamp. The rest of the lights were out because he hated paying Savannah Electric and Power one penny more than he had to. That was Jim.

I would guess that Jim was in his early to mid-60s, and that he held the sensibilities of many Southern white men of his generation – that is, that he was opposed to interracial dating. But, if he ever had a problem with a black man and a white woman hanging out together in his establishment, I never knew it. There were many nights when Diane and I were the only people in the place. We would shoot pool for an hour or two, drink beer and talk with Jim. I think watching us together brought Jim a great deal of amusement, and maybe even some joy. We even invited him to our wedding, and I think he was honored. One of my favorite memories of that day was hearing Jim proudly proclaiming to Diane's parents that she and I had "fallen in love on his pool table." A picture of the three of us taken that day sat on Jim's bar for many years afterward. A framed copy of the picture sits on a shelf in our living room.

On weekends, Jim's would attract a cross section of Savannah. From the young and boisterous Savannah College of Art and Design (SCAD) students to the downright eccentrics to the odd yuppie trying to tolerate everyone, the place was an interesting mix of people. And Diane and I were right in the midst of them, often known as "that pool-shooting couple." We would play doubles matches against anybody, and we amassed a pretty good winning percentage. We made so many great memories at Jim's.

During her visit to Jim's that holiday season, Diane decided to make a mini-cassette tape for me. On it she had various friends and patrons from Jim's record messages of support and goodwill to me. She sent it to me as a present, and I thought it was awesome. As I listened to the various messages from my desert home, I laughed my ass off.

Also enclosed in this wonderful care package were some blank cassettes which, by February, I had yet to make use of. As the ground war approached, I felt compelled to change that. In my letters, I thought I'd expressed my feelings pretty well. But I still felt that wasn't quite enough. I did not want to go into battle with anything left unsaid to my wife. And I personally wanted to say it – I wanted Diane to hear my voice. Just in case I did not make it back, I wanted her to hear me say "I love you" one more time.

So, on one clear evening I walked out into the desert alone. By the light of a star-filled sky and a crescent moon, I spoke from my heart into that mini-cassette recorder. I had not planned or practiced what I was going to say. I just spoke to my wife (although rambled may be a more accurate description). As the words and emotions poured out, a great sense of relief washed over me. I finished talking about 35 minutes after I started, and it was as if the weight of the world was lifted from my shoulders.

I was emotionally drained, but I never felt more energized. The simple act of verbalizing everything to Diane also left me with a profound new sense of acceptance about my future. I knew that whatever came next was to a very large extent out of my hands, and the acknowledgement of that lack of control was liberating beyond belief. I had told the person I love the most how I felt. And if the end of my time on earth was at hand, I was prepared to meet my maker.

I mailed the tape a week or two before our attack, not knowing what Diane's reaction would be on the other side of the world, in Columbus, Georgia. I did not find out until after I was home. Diane told me that she listened to the tape one time, cried her eyes out for 20 minutes, threw it in a drawer and vowed never to listen to it again. In 20 years she never has. Reading these letters again has been an emotional journey for both of us. It has not been easy. Listening to the tape again would only compound the pain.

As for me, I have never listened to the tape. I never have liked the sound of my own voice, but beyond that I'm not sure what purpose it would serve to recall those difficult emotions. Nevertheless, as I write these words, I am still conflicted. I'm curious sometimes about the precise words I used, and how I said them, what my pitch and tone was like, if I sounded sad, confident or resolute. Who knows if one day that curiosity will actually compel me to listen.

Still, in happier times Diane and I have been able to joke about it all. We've even dubbed that particular recording as the "Death Tape," for obvious reasons. The nickname has stuck for all of these years.

At the same time, just writing about the Death Tape reminds me that I caused Diane a lot of pain with it. But, despite the hurt that I unintentionally inflicted, I have no regrets. I needed to make that tape.

And having done so, I was ready to face whatever came next, whatever that might be. What I did know for certain was that all of this would be over soon enough. I would either be returning to Diane upright and unscathed, scarred but still breathing, or in a flag-draped coffin.

Somehow, some way, I would soon be going home.

FEBRUARY 1991

Dear Diane,

We have moved 480 km to a position within 10 miles of the Iraqi border. Within the next two weeks things could get very interesting. I was commander of one of the convoys up here. I led a total of 34 vehicles on an all night road march to our current location. It was an interesting experience.

The Air Force seems to be kicking some major ass. As far as I'm concerned they can continue for as long as they like. I'm still hoping that a ground war will not be necessary. Too many variables... I know that it's not likely that air alone will be decisive. But I continue to remain hopeful.

I'm doing fine. My spirits and confidence are still high. I'm just praying for a quick resolution to all of this. I want to come home.

I think you are right when you say that this will make us closer. I will appreciate you more than I ever did. And I know that we have lots of happy times together ahead of us. I also think that you are right when you say that we should stay out of the Michelle/Scott turmoil. I just hope that they will be okay.

I got your tape but have not listened to it yet. I don't know why not. I'm sure I will listen to it within the next day or two. Things have been so topsy-turvy lately. I just have not had the mindset to sit down and content myself. But I will. Don't worry.

A week at home in bed with you sounds wonderful. A cruise sounds wonderful. Sitting down to one of your meals sounds wonderful. Being anywhere but here sounds wonderful.

DEAR DIANE

I will try to write daily until we are committed to action. Don't worry. I will be fine. Just keep the faith. Take care and be good.

Love always,
Stephen

3 FEBRUARY, 1991
1715 HRS.

Dear Diane,

I am trying to keep my promise by writing to you as much as I possibly can until the action starts for me. Not the kind of "action" that I'm looking forward to, if you know what I mean. ☺ But don't worry. My spirits are still high. Now that the war has started, each passing day brings me one day closer to being at home.

Do you know a doctor by the name of Nadja West? She normally works family practice at Martin. Right now she heads up the ATLS[41] team that is with 2-69. I mentioned your name to her and it seemed to ring a bell with her. Anyway, she seems to be very nice. I have decided to subscribe to Fortune magazine. It has really got some good aspects to it. I just dropped the business reply card in the mail. If I take an extremely optimistic view, I may be home by the time the first issue arrives. Note that the emphasis is on extremely optimistic.

I hope that you have given more thought to your career post staff nursing. I know that you are an excellent nurse. I really do. But you can't want to do that forever. I know that $32k is a decent salary, but you are worth so much more. With the right training you would be a great administrator given your vast experience. You could also be a terrific teacher at the university level. I know that you have given this some thought. At least I hope so. We will be going through a lot of changes in the next 2-3 years: having a baby, me leav-

---

[41] ATLS: The abbreviation for Advanced Trauma Life Support.

ing the Army. I just don't want you to be doing patient care after you are 40.

I would still like to get you a new cocktail ring as a reward for performing like a Trojan warrior during the last 6 months. We could trade up from the one you got last year for Christmas. Your original engagement ring is something we should keep. Years from now when we are financially well off we can look at it and think back to our humble beginnings. I thought about getting you a lady Rolex. But I just don't think that wearing a Rolex means as much to you as it does to me.

I know that you are doing great and wonderful things with the money: i.e., our investments. Something to think about: a slush fund for our travel/party money. We are gonna need it baby. By the way, did my Chevy Chase Gold Card come in yet?

Regarding Valentine's Day, I don't know if this will get to you in time. But you have to know that you are my one and only Valentine. And that you occupy my entire heart.

Love always,

Stephen

5 FEBRUARY, 1991

1715 HRS.

Dear Diane,

I feel like I am drowning in a sea of shitheads. The desert has not gotten to me. The separation has not gotten to me. The prospect of impending combat has not gotten to me.

What has gotten to me is the total lack of support that the leadership of this battalion gives. I now know for certain that as soon as I'm back at Ft. Benning

DEAR DIANE

I'm getting out of this fucking place.

Something that happened this morning nearly pushed me over the edge. Let me give you the background info. A few nights ago, we received a Red Cross message on a soldier in A Company whose loco parentis grandfather had died. I immediately called that message to the company in accordance with proper procedures. A day or two passed with no action. So I asked the company 1st Sergeant about it. He seemed completely clueless, but said he would investigate. It turns out that the soldier who received the message simply did not pass it to the company leadership. After this revelation the leadership got involved and we proceeded to process the soldier's leave paperwork. This morning in the Command and Staff meeting S. asked me about it. When I tried to explain he chewed my ass, claiming that it was my fault and my responsibility, totally absolving the leadership of the company of any responsibility. I suppose I could have followed up sooner. But, still... I didn't really get pissed until he said that if I could not handle the responsibility he would get someone else, and then left. Needless-to-say, I stood there fuming. I was so mad I could have killed someone. But, I let myself cool off for about ten minutes and went back to him and said, "Sir, if you are that disappointed in my performance then I need to know, and you can relieve me as you see fit." This time he gave me the dear old dad routine where he tried to explain to me the error of my ways and began giving me "helpful hints" on how to be a better S-1. This little song and dance pissed me off more than the ass chewing. When he was chewing my ass I looked him eyeball to eyeball. When he was giving me the old soft shoe I could not bear to. So much phoniness. So much horseshit.

I don't trust these guys. And I am getting the fuck out of this battalion as soon as I can. I honestly feel like these guys are sitting around trying to think of a reason. Fuck these guys.

I had to take a break to go to the TOC[42] and brief S. on another incident. But, I am back now. In the interim the mail came in. I got a letter from you, a package from Ann Brown and Ken and a very sweet letter from Michelle. It has put me in a better mood.

Still nothing changes. The same stupid fucks are doing the same stupid things. I have had it.

I would like to end this letter on a good note. So, I will. I am grateful for all of the friends we have who have written to me and who are calling you to show their support. We are lucky to have them. And we are lucky to have each other.

I will always love you.

Stephen

6 FEBRUARY, 1991
0745 HRS.

Dear Diane,

After a good night's sleep I am feeling a little better now. The anger has subsided but the feelings remain. I will do my job and maintain a low profile until all of this is over.

Unless, of course, I am pushed too far. Then I will tell S., R. and everyone else to get fucked. If I were offered the chance to command right now I would refuse it. I don't want anything to do with these guys. When the command climate changes, this might be a good battalion. I think it is in my best interest to go somewhere else until R. and F. are gone. Then I might consider coming back to command a company in this place.

---

[42] TOC: Army abbreviation for Tactical Operations Center.

DEAR DIANE

What I'd like to do is be a TAC[43] officer at the Officer Candidate School (OCS). I think that it would be a great challenge and a lot of fun. Ft. Benning is the only place where that opportunity is available. As a tanker instead of an infantryman, it would be a unique experience. I will aggressively pursue that option upon my return. The only drawback is that as an OCS TAC I would probably have to shave my mustache. ☺ Oh well!

Did I tell you that I got a letter from Uncle Oscar and Aunt Elaine? It was very nice. I wrote them back immediately.

Are you still maintaining a list of things that I miss? I have two more things to add: watching C-Span and McLaughlin.

How is the book hunt going? I hope that it is enjoyable for you. It's okay if you don't get everything. Just maintain the list. We will have fun looking together when I get back.

How are things on the fertility front? Are you looking forward to one day being a mommy? ☺

Not much more to report at this time. I will continue to try to drop you a line daily until the action begins for us.

Take care and be good.

Love always,
Stephen

---

[43] TAC: Abbreviation for Teach Assess and Counsel, which is a type of instructor at Officer Candidate School.

6 FEBRUARY, 1991
1900 HRS.

Dear Diane,

I finally listened to the tape today. It was wonderful. Everyone sounded really good. It is really nice to know that people care. As I have stated before, we are very lucky to have the friends that we have. I especially like Diane Hicklin's comment. It was a nice ego boost. I could tell that you were a little drunk when you said something to the effect of that you wanted to f--- me when I got home. I found that to be quite amusing and uncharacteristic for you.

Believe it or not, things right now are pretty calm for us. But I know that it is the calm before the storm. When G-day arrives things are going to get real interesting. But, I won't dwell on that.

I am still doing fine both mentally and physically. Despite the fact that I have been pissed off for the last few days, I know that I can deal with it.

I was glad to hear in the tape the determination in your voice with regard to your weight loss. I'm sure that you look just beautiful and that you have men fawning all over you. But, I am not jealous. You deserve that kind of attention.

I am grateful that we have such a strong relationship. All around me I learn of marriages in trouble. Spouses not writing to each other and people running around on each other. The casualties from this operation will be more than just what happens on the ground here.

I've got no problem with you asking your dad for some cash for my new car. Saving on interest is a good idea. Maximizing our investment cash is also a good idea. More and more you are thinking like me.

DEAR DIANE

If this arrives before Ed and Ruta do just tell them how much I wish that I could be there.

From the tone of your last letter you and little Sandy had a good time. I'm sure that it was nice to see her.

On the tape you said that you were considering going back to school. I think that is good. You are a talented person and if you applied yourself you could do anything.

What do you think of these names:

> *GIRL: Ivey Katherine Bradshaw*
> *BOY: Quentin Randolph Bradshaw*

I guess you knew all along that the Elmo Dwayne was a no go. ☺ Your plan for the timing of your procedure is good. I wish I could give you a timeline for my return, but I can't.

Regarding the things that I have written to you about in recent days, I feel the storm has passed. Don't worry. You know that I am a survivor. This morning in the command and staff meeting I retaliated in kind. But it was in a very tactful and eloquent manner. But the message was crystal clear: "Don't fuck with me." You would have been proud. My feelings about this place have not changed. And I will ruthlessly pursue the fastest means out of here upon my return.

Not much more to report at this time. Take care and be good.

Love always,
Stephen

FEBRUARY 1991

Dear Diane,

Another day in paradise. Not a lot going on. Still waiting for the time when the big ground attack will begin. I believe that the ground war will be short (2-4 weeks) and very violent. Many will be hurt. Some will die. These are the grim realities. Hopefully, our side will fare better than the enemy. As G-day (ground day) approaches, I am not gripped by fear. I know what has to be done. I'll do it and I will come home to you.

I would still like for you to find me a complete DCU uniform to send (both trousers and shirt). Make sure that you get all of my stuff sewed on. If the timing is right, it will get here in time before we depart for home. My other ones are kind of trashed and I want to look good for the flight home. ☺

I have another book request to add to the list. Breaking Barriers by Carl T. Rowan. It is supposed to be pretty good and I would like to read it.

I'll keep this one short. You know how much I love you. Just hang in there. I'll be home before you know it.

Love,
Stephen

DEAR DIANE

Dear Diane,

Your letters are getting to me, which at this point is very fortunate. I need them now more than ever. The one that I got from you today was dated 25 January 1991. In it you stated that the last letter that you had received from me was dated 6 January. I am continuing to write. The letters should be getting to you.

You are right when you say that the waiting is making me a little crazy. But I would rather wait than rush into anything in a foolhardy manner. I will wait for as long as it takes.

I'm glad that you got your leave granted for Ed and Ruta's visit. You guys will have a great time together.

What is the name of the attractive blond that worked with you on 2BA? She was a Captain, as I recall, who lived in Whisperwood for awhile. The reason I'm asking is that a friend of mine, Jeff Williams, is interested in making contact with her. I gave him a description and he seemed interested. Now, you know my feelings on getting into the match-making business. But, Jeff is a nice guy and we are in a war zone.

I hope the tone of some of my recent letters did not upset you. But, I had a run of about 5 really shitty days. I don't know what it was. But, I hope that it's all behind me now. Your decision on the CD was fine. You have become quite the financial decision maker. On taxes I am almost inclined to tell you to just knock it out to get it over with. But it is your decision.

I just read an interesting article in Army Times about the job hunt for officers getting out. It did not paint a rosy picture overall. But it did state that guys at my end are faring much better than guys at the higher end. I'm not worried at all. I have until 17 March 1994 at the latest to find what I want. When I do get actively involved in the civilian job hunt I think I will use one of those recruiting firms in addition to pursuing my own leads.

Ideally, I would prefer to go from the Army to a job in Georgia state government for about two years, before going corporate. This would give me a chance to sow some future political seeds, plus use them to pursue a high paying job in the corporate world. We'll see.

As I have stated before, I'm glad that you have given some consideration to your career as well. You are a talented person. Don't sell yourself short.

People are continuing to write to me. And I am very grateful. I still have not received any package from you with the magazines. I guess it is still on the way.

Don't worry. I'm fine. And I will continue to be fine. Take care and be good.

Love always,
Stephen

17 FEBRUARY, 2009
0830 HRS.

Dear Diane,

I apologize for my sporadic writing of late. It's been a combination of being busy and not having the mindset to write. Today is G-day minus 4 days. We have been hearing rumblings of late that Saddam may be starting to reconsider his tough stance. A month of continuous bombing is enough to alter anyone's perspective. Well, he has got 4 days to make a move, otherwise his army will be crushed. I won't dwell on this subject. We'll just see what happens.

With regard to my credit, you are absolutely right. I don't know what is fucking it up. It will be high on my priority list of things to unscrew when I get back.

With regard to the new car, I think I have made up my mind on the Integra. I am almost willing to let you go ahead and buy it as soon as you get definite word that we are on the way home. I know that you are probably reluctant to do that, but you know what I like, and I trust your judgement completely. What I am afraid of is that as soon as we get back into town everyone is going to start jacking up prices again. It is bad to think that dealers would try to stick it to soldiers after all we have been through. But, when it comes to money I don't put anything past anybody. Also, getting money from your dad is a good idea. If you were able to offer a dealer $10,000 in cash you would probably be able to drive off the lot in a car.

I'm glad that Mike and Michelle are staying in contact with each other. It is good to have friends. By the way, I hope you had a good time in New Orleans. Did anyone tell you that you have Bruce Springsteen lips? ☺

In recent weeks I have formed a very close friendship with a woman named Jane Stewart. She is a Captain who works in Brigade S-1. She is from Cairo, GA, which she pronounces CARO, and she is very nice. Her husband is stationed at Ft. Benning. He works for the post CSM[44]. I really can't explain why we have become so close. Maybe it's just being here. She is very easy to talk to. And we have talked about lots of things, including our relationships with our spouses. I know that we will remain friends when all of this is over. I can't wait for you to meet her. I think that you will really like each other.

I'm glad that people say nice things about our apartment. I know that you have done a wonderful job in decorating. I'm sure it is just beautiful, like my honey. It is nice knowing that I will have a comfortable place to come home to.

---

[44] CSM: Abbreviation for Command Sergeant Major.

My letter flow has continued to be good. Unfortunately, I think I have reached the point where I won't be able to write back to everyone who writes to me. When you talk to people, please tell them that I still appreciate everything that everyone has done. Tell them to please continue. And tell them that I will write again as soon as I can.

Thank you again for being my wife. I am the luckiest man on earth.

Love always,
Stephen

p.s. I got your care packages. Also, if you are going to send me one magazine, make it Atlanta.

20 FEBRUARY, 1991
1300 HRS.

Dear Diane,

I apologize for the sporadic nature of my letters lately. Things, as you might expect, are getting a little more tense. We had started the countdown to G-day. We are currently at G minus 3 and holding. How long we will be holding is anyone's guess. The feverish diplomatic activity that has been going on of late has kinda thrown a monkey wrench into everyone's plans. Again, I don't relish the idea of going into Iraq. I just want this to be over. Don't worry. I will hang in there for the duration. I have mentally prepared myself to stay here for a year. Naturally, I am hoping that I am not here that long. But, I am ready to go the distance.

It has rained two nights within the last week, which has really sucked. But, overall the weather is starting to improve. It is getting warmer. Within another month or two it will be downright hot again. By then I hope that we are

DEAR DIANE

at least out of these MOPP suits.

The other day I was talking to my friend Jane about home. We both agree that the thought of home is like a spot on a very distant horizon. This desert is home for now. Our day-to-day grind is our life. It is just hard for me to believe that half a year has gone by. In one sense it seems that time has flown. In another sense it seems as if I have been here forever.

So much has happened in the past six months. And I know that it will get worse before it gets better. Whether there is war or peace (for the ground forces that is) I know that I won't leave this desert wilderness completely unscathed.

When I get home I just want us to be together. However, (and I am sure you can appreciate this) I will want some time alone. You know how much I love solitude. I just have not had any in a very long time. There are always other people around. Always somebody wanting something. So don't be surprised if one day I just get in the car and go... nowhere in particular. Just go... I know you will understand. One of your most wonderful qualities has always been your maturity. I love you for it.

Jane asked me the other day if it was weird or wrong for her to want to be alone also. She has only been married for a little over a year and is worried about how her husband might react. I told her that it was normal. It seemed to make her feel better. We even joked that when I was off alone and she was off alone that we would run into each other.

I said if I saw her first I would go the other way. ☺ As you may have gathered, she and I have become good friends. We talk about everything, including marriage. Now that I am an old married man I feel qualified to talk knowingly on the subject. ☺ I know that the two of you will like each other.

So today is the day that Ed and Ruta are to arrive. I know that you will have a good time. You know I wish I could be there.

Please pass along to Michelle my deepest sympathy on the loss of her father. It had to be a shock. I hope she holds up all right.

Not much more to report at this time. I'll write as much as I can prior to G-day. I love you.

Always,

Stephen

20 FEBRUARY, 1991
1430 HRS.

Dear Diane,

You may have heard that some people got a chance to make phone calls. They did. I decided that I would not call you. Right now I am in the right frame of mind to do battle. I have got the edge and I am trying hard not to peak too soon. I think that my time table is on course. Talking to you would have taken me off track. I would have started missing you more and it would have messed me up. There will be time for us to talk to each other when all of this is over. I know that you understand.

I just thought of something. I love the picture that you sent to me of you, Liz and Mrs. Butler. You really look beautiful. Really.

I have been thinking a lot about my (our) political future. My mind is pretty much made up that my first campaign will be for an Atlanta City Council seat in 1997. I am gonna have to start making moves as soon as I return. I suspect that we will spend a lot of weekends in Atlanta scoping out neighborhoods and making our presence known. One of the first things I'm going to do is become a member of the Atlanta Lawn Tennis Association. I can also see that one major setback on the campaign trail is the fact that I am not an Atlanta native. In fact I'll be a Johnny-come-lately. We need to do everything we can to diffuse that. Being at Ft. Benning will make access to Atlanta a little easier. Something to consider.

The volume of letters from you lately has been wonderful. Please keep it up. I need it. Once again let me tell you that I am extremely proud of the way that you have conducted yourself throughout this whole ordeal.

I can't wait to get home so that I can rip your clothes off and do unspeakable acts with you. ☺

Til' then…

Love always,
Stephen

22 FEBRUARY, 1991
1910 HRS.

Dear Diane,

This may be the last letter of mine for awhile, if this one even gets to you. As it stands right now, at 0600 hours on 25 February we will launch our portion of the ground offensive. The last six months have come down to this. We are about to go on one hell of a ride. By the time this gets to you we will be decisively engaged. If we kick major ass, the ground fighting may even be over. So, I don't feel like I am violating any security by telling you the following: You may have heard General Powell on TV say that our goal is to cut the Iraqi Army off and then kill it. The mission of the 24th ID with the 197th Brigade is to cut it off. We will move over 500 km and set up blocking positions in the Euphrates River Valley. We will be on the only high speed route back to Baghdad. It ought to be interesting. I am afraid, but not so much. I am just ready to get on with it. I fully expect to be home within 60-90 days.

When the news comes that the ground attack has started, you will be with Ed and Ruta. It is comforting to know that you will be with people who really care.

I got a really sweet letter from Linda (as in Linda and Joel) today. It made me think again about how lucky we are to have such caring friends. I hope to be able to thank them all in person upon my return.

My hope is that we can execute this mission with minimum loss of life. I know that when the 197th/2-69 sustains its first casualty it will be a shocking experience for all of us.

In the time that we have been here I have not come up with a new or innovative way to tell you that I love you. In spite of that, I think you know how I feel. You are the best wife that a man could ever hope to have. And I am very grateful.

Continue to save money aggressively. I have enclosed a newspaper clipping of the Acura that I like. Again, it may be a very good idea to make the purchase prior to my return to save money. You know what I like. I trust your judgement. I don't want you to feel that just because it's primarily going to be my car that I have to be knee deep in the selection process. It's just transportation to me. I don't think that I get as attached to automobiles as you do. My advice is that when you get positive info on when I will be home, go ahead and execute. If you have any other doubts, remember this: Our wedding day was the most important event in our lives to date. You handled all of the details for that and it turned out beautifully. I think that the purchase of a car pales by comparison.

I will end this letter on a positive note, so hang on to this thought. I love you always.

Stephen

On the afternoon of Feb. 24, 1991, the ground phase
of Operation Desert Storm began for our unit.

eight

CEASEFIRE

I wish I could report that I did something heroic during my time in the Gulf War – that I was engaged in a major firefight, that I killed several enemy soldiers, that I saved the lives of my comrades. That would certainly be a satisfying ending to this story. But it would not be true. The reality was that enemy resistance in our area of operation was almost zero, and those circumstances didn't lend themselves to much battlefield heroism.

Saddam Hussein had concentrated his forces in and around Kuwait, probably not thinking that we would actually breach the territorial sovereignty of Iraq. So, he had no defenses in our sector of operations. The first three days of the ground war were essentially a blur as we advanced well over 300 kilometers into Iraq without encountering any Iraqi resistance. But on the afternoon of February 27, 1991, that changed. At approximately 12:30 hours I found myself on the ground about 50 meters away from the protection of my armored personnel carrier, directing some support vehicles toward our tanks.

A two-lane paved road that ran from the northwest to the southeast would serve as the primary route for our vehicles. Our tanks were approximately five kilometers to the southeast. Radio traffic indicated that they were preparing for an assault on an Iraqi airfield to the northwest. We needed to get the support vehicles to the location to refuel and rearm as needed, and I was in charge of that operation.

The last fuel truck had cleared my location when suddenly an approximately 2½–ton truck appeared on the road, heading toward us from the northwest. It was not one of ours.

I can only assume that the driver of this foreign vehicle took note of what was going on in front of him, because he came to a sudden stop about

800 meters from us. Needless to say, the situation had me more than a little curious.

But curiosity quickly turned into fear as I saw several men jump from the back of the truck, moving with what I perceived to be hostile intentions. My first thought was, "Oh shit – this is it." And I immediately dropped down behind a berm, upholstered my Beretta 9mm pistol and moved the selector switch from safe to fire.

My fear began to mount as I soon realized that those bad guys would have to get pretty close before that 9mm pistol would do me any good. I figured I would have to make every shot count. Given what was unfolding, I was remarkably calm.

But, make no mistake, I was scared. I yelled at the guys on my vehicle, "We've got a fucking problem here!" Two of my soldiers armed with M-16 rifles joined me on the ground. We were ready to fight. Additionally, our vehicle had a small machine gun on the skate ring, so I thought we had enough firepower to give our opponents a serious problem. Of course, we had no idea what might be behind them.

Just then one of our M-88 recovery vehicles, also equipped with a machine gun on the skate ring, closed on our position. I pointed to the truck and the machine gun was aimed in that direction. With our makeshift force in place, we opened fire.

The bad guys quickly realized that they were outgunned, and I saw a few of them, I don't remember how many, run back toward their vehicle, which, in turn, did a 180 and took off in the opposite direction. Maybe we hit one of them. Maybe we didn't. Regardless, I was not going to stick around to find out. With that I ran back toward my vehicle, essentially dove in the back and yelled to my driver that "we need to get the fuck out of here."

Just then I heard one of my sergeants (who shall remain nameless) screaming "Oh my god, we're all going to die! We're all going to die!" I could not believe what I was witnessing. Younger soldiers were ready to go to battle with the enemy while this senior sergeant was blubbering like a baby. I was furious.

Moreover, this sergeant had a death grip on the hand microphone for our radio, and we needed to report the incident immediately to the tactical operation center – if there was more trouble behind these guys, we had to get support fast. Without regard for niceties or decorum, I snatched the mic out of the sergeant's hand. I was sweating. My heart was pounding. This odd combination of fear and anger had overtaken me. So I took a few seconds to compose myself, and with all the calm I could muster (which was not very much), I got on the radio and reported what had happened. After our adrenaline stopped surging, we eventually got back on task and moved in the direction of our tanks.

We weren't sure if this little skirmish would foretell more to come. Now that we were deep in Iraq, maybe more engagements with enemy soldiers were just around the corner. We began to move east toward the town of Basra.

In the eastern area of operations, allied forces were taking on Iraqi forces in Kuwait. As Iraqi forces retreated in the face of overwhelming American firepower, the battle plan called for them to be cut off en route back to Baghdad in the north. The retreating Iraqi units would run into us – the 24th Infantry Division and its approximately 20,000 soldiers. And that's exactly what happened. Saddam made the determination that his forces were defeated, and they more or less surrendered. Less than 24 hours after our little skirmish, Operation Desert Shield/Storm was essentially over.

Even now, all these years later, the receipt of the ceasefire order strikes me as almost surreal. In the wee hours of February 28 as we were moving east, I received a radio message indicating that President Bush had ordered a ceasefire that would be effective in a few hours. I couldn't believe it. I was still a little jacked up from the previous day's incident. Also, I – like everyone else – was sleep deprived, so I was probably not thinking very clearly. I honestly thought I had not heard the message correctly. But I had. I just could not believe that in a few hours the war would officially be over.

It was not until I had returned home when I saw images of the "highway of death" – the moniker for a major highway that the Iraqi forces were trying to use as an escape route from the onslaught of allied forces. Major news agencies captured the unmitigated destruction of Iraqi vehicles, equipment and soldiers, and broadcast them worldwide. That prompted President Bush to end hostilities before our attack began to look gratuitous. Of course, I did not know any of that at the time. As the ceasefire took hold, I felt a sense of great relief and joy. We had survived. Even so, it still seemed unreal.

What I still marvel at is how quickly we reverted from warriors to humanitarians. Most of the Iraqis I saw were either dead or prisoners of war, of which we had taken on many. But we treated them well. An individual whom we would have fired at without hesitation the day before was someone we were trying to help a day later because our Commander-In-Chief had told us it was over. It is a testament to our ideals as Americans, and it makes me very proud.

Combat operations were over, our mission objectives had been achieved, and we had done so with limited casualties. But, for the loved ones of the 148 soldiers who died in battle, the war was devastating. Those feelings were manifested again fairly recently. On August 2, 2009, the remains of Captain Michael Scott Speicher were recovered. He was the first person to die in Operation Desert Storm. The news brought all the memories, all the pain, all the tension, all the heartache back to me.

I was safe, though, and upon news of the ceasefire order, I could begin to turn my attention to thoughts of home.

As my comrades and I started the process of gathering and packing up our personal items, I wondered what I would do with the letters from Diane. She was almost as prolific as I was, and I had saved the dozens of letters she'd written me since I'd been in the desert. But I knew transporting them, along with all my other gear, would be difficult.

So, one day before we left, I gathered her letters and buried them in the desert. With the sands blowing around me, I stood there alone, thanking my Creator for blessing me with such a wonderful wife. Diane's letters had served their purpose, and it somehow seemed appropriate that they should remain in the area of the world where they had done the most good. Even so, I sometimes wish I had them now.

Within a week or so of the ceasefire, we returned to Saudi Arabia and stayed in the city of Dhahran. For the first time in months, we had access to actual showers and real toilets. Believe me, until you have gone without those everyday luxuries it's impossible to realize how wonderful they are.

To be sure, the atmosphere among our soldiers was demonstrably lighter than it had been in a long time. One day while walking around our compound I saw a guy wearing a T-shirt that read "A Patriot Missile Saved My Ass" with the date of the counterattack on one of Saddam's scuds. I doubled over with laughter right there on the street.

A few weeks later, we were boarding commercial airplanes, heading back to the United States. The mood on our return flights was completely different than it had been on the flights to the Middle East. We had done our duty and we were victorious. And the American people shared in this victory. This was underscored in the most thunderous way when we had our first encounter with American citizens on American soil in the town of Bangor, Maine, on March 29, 1991.

I wrote about the experience in a newspaper piece several months after our return.[45] It was like nothing I had ever experienced before or since. We were greeted like heroes by the people in Bangor, and the whole scene moved me in the most profound way. I will never forget the little girl, maybe five or six years old, who broke away from her mom and walked up to me with her arms wide open for a hug. It presented me with a photo opportunity that I simply could not pass up. Her mom took a photo that I still have today (in the photo section of this book).

A few hours and a few delays later, we landed in Ft. Benning, Georgia. We were home. The post commander shook hands with every soldier as we

---

[45] Please see Appendix B for the full article that ran in the *Shawano Evening Leader*.

deplaned, which I thought was a classy gesture as our loved ones waited in a hanger just off the landing strip.

I approached the cheering crowd, searching the faces for Diane. Then I saw her... my wonderful wife, whose love and support had sustained me throughout the entire ordeal. After eight months apart, Diane was almost within reach. But, believe it or not she was not the first to hug me. Our dear friend Michelle actually reached me first. She was closer to me as I approached, and we shared a brief moment that was actually very sweet. Seconds later I embraced my wife, and that moment was as surreal as the months that had preceded it.

It is very difficult to accurately capture the array of emotions that I felt in that instant. I don't remember crying. But I do remember feeling pure joy. I was in a state of euphoria and stunned disbelief. I was actually home, 13 days before our fourth wedding anniversary. We left the air field and got into my brand-new car, a 1991 Acura Integra, which we'd discussed in my letter, but which I'd not yet even seen. Diane drove us to our apartment in Columbus. I don't recall what we talked about on the drive or if I even said much at all.

Diane had made one of my favorite meals – seafood and angel hair pasta – for dinner, but I barely touched it. I guess I was still in some weird state of disequilibrium. But I was overjoyed to be home.

The next day Diane did something that was very wise. She had scheduled herself to work that day and left me alone in our apartment. I thought it was smart at the time, but in 20 years of retrospection I have come to regard her decision as brilliant. Reentry to one's life following an extended deployment is difficult. It takes time. Having well-meaning loved ones in your face all at once is not always a good thing. You spend months living in a tent in the desert in a desolate, sweltering place, an existence that's so far removed from what you know but yet over time becomes your reality, your new normal. Then you are thrust back into your real life, which has in fact become the old normal. It takes some major adjustment. You need time and space to regain your bearings.

But many people don't understand this and make the mistake of smothering the recently returned soldier. Maybe with her clinical experience as a nurse, Diane had special insight into this and planned accordingly. But whatever the reason, I was grateful to be by myself the day after returning home.

When I left for Iraq the previous August, we weren't fully settled into our apartment. Eight months later, wandering around it, I realized I didn't know where anything was. So, I spent hours exploring, looking in closets and looking in drawers just to get a sense of my surroundings, of my home. It was very calming and very enlightening.

Later I wandered around our apartment complex. It was a pretty spring day and being outside felt nice. As I was standing by the duck pond watching those beautiful little creatures glide through the water, I think the reality that I was actually home finally began to sink in. My strange adventure in the Middle East was actually over. By the time Diane got home from work that day, I was starting to feel more like myself again.

In the immediate aftermath of Operation Desert Shield/Storm, the best thing in the world to be was a soldier who had been there. I admit without shame that I parlayed my "war veteran" status into free beer in bars from Savannah to Madison, Wisconsin, to San Francisco. It's not like I had a sign around my neck advertising the fact. People who didn't know me just somehow figured it out. Maybe it was my haircut, maybe it was my demeanor, maybe it was my vocabulary – I honestly don't know. And of course, compared to what our soldiers are dealing with today, calling myself a war veteran was a bit of a stretch. Still, it was nice to be appreciated. And I'm never one to turn down free beer.

I was often asked "How was it?" My response was usually the same: "It sucked." Succinct, always delivered without aplomb, but rather with a contrite gratitude for just being home in one piece. Honestly, the ground war was over so fast that it hardly registered. But, waiting around in the desert for all of those months nearly drove me crazy, and I had no qualms about telling people so.

Once I returned home, I began thinking about what my future would look like. I'd already been considering leaving the military, and I've always been interested in public service. In my letters to Diane I'd written about my possible political aspirations. While that interest remains, my name has yet to appear on a ballot. As I was finishing graduate school in 1998, I gave running for office somewhat serious consideration. But the timing was just not right. Subsequently, such thoughts have been put on the shelf, though the idea still tugs at me sometimes.

In 2001, I was honored to be appointed by Georgia's then-governor, Roy Barnes, to a state board that oversaw the certification of water plant operators. I held the position for more than two years and I found it both educational and rewarding. I also developed a love for teaching. Since 2005, I have been an instructor in the public policy school at Georgia State University. I get a tremendous amount of joy engaging with my students and learning from them.

The subject of children comes up a lot in my letters as well. I love children, and I always assumed I would be a father some day. It did not happen, though, and for the most part I have come to terms with that. Diane and I tried very hard in the early '90s to have children as I was nearing the end of my military service, but it wasn't in the cards for us. Diane had two miscarriages, which is one of the most horrible experiences I believe a human being can go through. I'm not sure I was ever happier than when she told me that she was pregnant the first time, and I don't think I ever felt more devastated than when she miscarried a few weeks later. After the second, we decided to stop, simply because the emotional roller coaster was just too much.

We opted not to try other measures to conceive. Diane was a trouper throughout the entire process, and for that she has my eternal respect and admiration. We thought about adopting for many years, but we never took steps to make that happen. I guess we were just enjoying our lives too much. Now, as age 50 is within sight for me, I think about what not having children means for our future. I wonder who will help take care of Diane and me in our later years, as selfish as that might sound. Regardless, I would like to find a way to play a positive role in the lives of children somehow. Our drive to conceive coincided with my decision to leave military service. I never saw myself as a career military officer, and as I approached my 30th birthday the time to make a change seemed right. Moreover, I knew that continued military service would mean future deployments and long periods of family separation. As I was growing up, my father was gone a lot due to his military service. He was doing his duty, and I'm proud of him and our family's military tradition. But my father and I were not close when I was growing up. And I didn't want that life for the children Diane and I were trying to have – I wanted to be around to watch them grow up. I spent my last 18 months on active duty, as an instructor at the Army officer candidate school. This was a wonderful experience, one that I may choose to write about at some point in the future.

In May 1993, I resigned my commission and left active military service.

In the summer of 1997, I was in Savannah for a visit. I had left active duty four years prior and was trying to make my way in the corporate world. One day, on a whim, I decided to drive past my old high school. I parked my car, got out and walked up to the chain link fence surrounding the parade field. As the hot Georgia sun beat down, I looked out over the field where I first learned to march, salute, and wear a military uniform – the place where my eventual trip to the desert had originated so many years prior.

There in the sunlight and silence, I was awash in a sea of memories. A smile formed on my lips and tears welled up in my eyes as I thought about everything I had gone through in my military career: the difficulty of being away from my wife, the uncertainty over whether I'd make it back, the friends and foes I'd made, good memories and not so good ones, the fear, the joy, the sense of pride – it all washed over me in a swell of emotion. I knew my time in the military was over, but I knew its impact on me would be life-lasting.

Nearly 20 years after I returned from my deployment in the Middle East, Diane and I are still together. As I would soon discover after my deployment, many divorces happen right after soldiers return home. Some marriages just don't survive with one spouse vastly changed from his or her wartime experience. (This consequence is yet another casualty of long deployments that I firmly believe is under-appreciated.) Down the road, other marriages simply fall apart, regardless of the strain of deployment. But I'm proud to say that Diane and I are still together. We're far from a perfect couple – I don't think they really exist anyway – and we've faced the same struggles that every long-term couple faces. But there is a subtle sense of accomplishment in staying with someone for as many years as we have, savoring the good times, and sticking it out through the bad (although I do admit that if I did more housework without being prompted, my esteem in my wife's eyes would rise considerably).

We continue to live in Atlanta, where, as this book was published, we've been for 17 years, and Diane is still working as a nurse while I'm teaching at a local university. On occasion, we even play a few games of pool together. Writing this book is just a small token of the gratitude and love I feel for my wife, whose remarkable strength during a very difficult time was and still is a profound sense of comfort and pride for me. Her support and love was my salvation, and I hope everyone who has taken the pledge to serve our great country has someone as wonderful as her behind them.

EPILOGUE

EPILOGUE

As I write these words, America is engaged in wars in both Iraq and Afghanistan, and thousands of fathers and mothers are separated from their children, friends from friends, families from families. Multiple, extended deployments have taken a tremendous toll on our soldiers and their families. It's an extraordinarily difficult problem, and my heart goes out to all who wait, wonder, worry and pray for loved ones in harm's way.

Of course, today's communication is much improved from when I served in Desert Shield/Desert Storm. The Internet, E-mail, Facebook, texting, satellite phones, and Skype all make connecting with loved ones much easier. In many ways these multiple platforms for staying in touch are wonderful. But – call me old school if you want – I find something very sweet and romantic about the exchange of the handwritten letters like those that passed between Diane and me during my deployment. And I would not trade it for anything. In our letters we articulated thoughts and feelings that we may never have communicated otherwise. As a result of that time apart, and despite the potential danger that was involved, we actually grew closer. And for that I am grateful.

My personal odyssey during the Gulf War as reflected in my letters to Diane is not meant to be representative of anyone else's experience. It is my own. But I have no doubt that commonalities exist. And they bind me not only to the soldiers who served with me, but also to soldiers of different war times. The sacrifices of families and friends are also shared across generations – it's not a hardship that's confined to one family unit, in a finite time period.

I'll leave it to others to write about the strategy involved in our deployment and our attack on the forces of Saddam Hussein. In fact, I highly recommend General H. Norman Schwarzkopf's *It Doesn't Take a Hero.* The book, published in 1992, is excellent, and in reading it I learned things about our mission there that I could not have possibly known as a lowly captain in the theater of operations. As far as movies go, a wonderful depiction of life for a soldier or marine at a tactical level during our deployment is provided in the 1999 picture *Jarhead,* based on the memoir by Anthony Swofford. It is a story that is funny and sad at the same time, and it's very well done.

Additionally, with nearly 20 years of reflection, I'd like to address several other issues. Was our mission to liberate Kuwait the right thing to do? Of course it was. Our cause was just. And our civilian and senior military leadership armed us with what we needed to be successful. Should we have gone further? Absolutely not. Exceeding our U.N. mandate would have fractured the coalition that had so skillfully been put together in support of our mission. Moreover, more of our soldiers would have been killed. Back then, toppling Saddam would have been a nice thing. But, it would have created a power vacuum that we would have had to fill. This would have meant being bogged down in Iraq for quite some time, which sounds familiar, doesn't it? (For the record, I have held this view since 1991.)

We did our jobs. We did significant damage to Saddam's war-making capability. We liberated the people of Kuwait. And, to some extent, we restored the esteem of our armed forces in the eyes of the American people. Not bad. I'll leave further analysis to others.

But on a more personal level, as I read through my letters I realized I sometimes expressed very sharp criticisms of certain institutions, practices and people. Right or wrong, it is what I felt at the time. To sanitize those sentiments 20 years later for the sake of sparing potential hurt feelings would be disingenuous. Still, I am sorry for any hurt feelings and I want to emphasize that I'm by no means perfect – far from it, in fact. Regardless of my criticisms, I have vast respect for every single person who served with me all those years ago.

Over dinner one night a few years after my return, Diane said something to me that took me by surprise. She told me that on the night of my return she watched me sleeping and wondered if I was the same man who had left for the desert all those months prior. This caught me off guard because I really had not thought about it in those terms.

I'm not sure what prompted her to bring it up on that particular evening. To be honest, I was actually a little offended. I guess it just struck me as an odd question, and I wondered why Diane couldn't just appreciate my being home instead of analyzing how I might have changed. So I asked her what she meant. She told me that she did think that I had changed, although she could not put her finger on just what was different about me.

As confused as I was by it, the conversation did get me thinking. I did not believe I was any different than before I left. My participation in Operation Desert Shield/Desert Storm in and of itself did not change my life in any profound way. In a larger sense, the war in the Persian Gulf was relatively quick and painless. The ground war only lasted for four days, after all. On a personal level, I did not suffer any physical or emotional harm, as difficult as the experience was. To my mind, I was essentially the same man.

Now, after nearly 20 years of hindsight, I have come to realize that the answer to the question of whether or not I was the same as before is a bit more complicated. The correct answer is both yes and no. Yes, for the aforementioned reasons. But, no because any experience of that magnitude is bound to change the individual who goes through it, even if those changes are not immediately self-evident. Whatever changes occurred in me as a result of my experience in the first Gulf War were on the whole changes for the better. I matured as a soldier and as a man. I gained invaluable self-knowledge and awareness. When my country called, I answered. And that's a good feeling to have about yourself.

Moreover, my respect and admiration for all who wear our nation's uniform(s) increased dramatically – feelings that remain to this day. Also, I have a much deeper respect and empathy for the loved ones who keep the faith and the home fires burning for the brave souls who are serving our country.

I was so proud to be among them. Not just for my service in Iraq, but for the entire seven years that I spent on active duty. It was the most formative experience of my entire professional life, and the world view I hold today was largely shaped by it.

To be certain, I was never a "super star" or "water walker." A general's stars were never to be a part of my future. But to paraphrase the renowned and controversial General Douglas MacArthur, I was just a soldier who tried to do his duty as God gave him the light to see that duty. If I was young again, I would do it all over.

Until recently, I traveled a good deal for work as a sales director. Almost every time I was in an airport, I would see young soldiers, especially around the holidays. At first, I would try to engage one or two of them and always thank them for their service. I'm sure my gestures of goodwill were appreciated. But, over time I began to just leave the soldiers alone. After all, I started to think that they were not items on display for the rest of us weary travelers. I began to think that just giving them their space was somehow more respectful of their service. But, that's just me.

Seeing those freshly scrubbed young faces so full of promise and possibility always makes me smile. But it makes me sad, too, and not just because of the fact that they might not return home. They are the best and the brightest that America has to offer, because they volunteer to do something that most of us are unwilling to do. While we share a common experience, I believe the soldiers of today face a much greater challenge than I did in 1990-1991. When I was in Iraq, we had a clear plan and a clear mission – to reverse Saddam Hussein's illegal invasion of Kuwait. And we went over there and executed that mission efficiently.

Today's ongoing missions in the Iraq and Afghanistan are much less definable – even as a former military officer I don't believe I have a clear understanding about what our current objectives are. Unfortunately, the soldiers bear the brunt of the difficulties that arise from mission creep. I know there are some who contend that not supporting the mission is equivalent to not supporting the soldiers, but I don't agree with that at all. In fact, I reject this line of reasoning completely. I just believe that too much is being asked of our soldiers today, especially in the absence of a clear and definable strategy for our military presence in Iraq and Afghanistan. Our troops today must play the roles of solider, diplomat and peacemaker, and in my mind that's asking way too much of these brave souls who risk their lives for our country.

Perhaps that's part of the reason I'm still so affected every time I see a soldier today. However conflicted I feel about the overall picture, though, I'm still awash in pride for these young men and women. We should embrace them and honor them in every way possible. And the people who love them, support them and await their return deserve no less. The gratitude that we – as a nation and as individuals – should show our military families cannot be overstated.

And if you, as a reader, take any message away from this book, I hope that's the one.

Acknowledgements

T his story belongs to Diane and me. But, this project would not have happened without the help of a number of great people.

First and foremost I must thank my wonderful editor Blane Bachelor. Blane is a very talented writer in her own right. Without the enthusiastic support that she displayed for this project from the very beginning, and the professionalism that she displayed throughout, this book would not have been possible. The many hours that we spent together working, laughing and sometimes crying have been a profound experience in my life. And her highly engaged participation made this endeavor demonstrably better than it otherwise would have been. I value the friendship that we have formed as a result of working on this together, and I hope that we remain friends for many years to come.

Ashley Bothwell is an incredibly talented graphic artist who came to my attention because of Blane. The first time I saw the design that eventually became the book jacket cover I was quite moved. After just one meeting with me she was able to capture the loneliness of the desert and the loneliness that was in my heart while I was deployed in a very beautiful and compelling image. Furthermore, I was impressed with all of her suggestions for the interior design as well. If you like the way this book looks and feels, thank Ashley. She possesses a talent that I am in awe of. And I am grateful to her for agreeing to be a part of this project.

I first met Caroline Farley when she was a fresh-faced student in one of my classes. I recognized her immense talent and potential then. And when I asked her to assist me in the marketing efforts for this project her enthusiastic response was very gratifying. But, Caroline has been much more than an assistant. She has in fact been the leader of our marketing efforts. And I have been very impressed with her diligence and devotion. To the extent that this book receives any attention beyond that of my small circle of friends and family ,I have Caroline to thank.

Josh Lamkin is an excellent photographer whose picture of me, which appears on the jacket and the website, make me look better than I actually do. That is no small accomplishment. Therefore, I am very grateful.

I also owe a huge debt of gratitude to Rodger Beyer and the entire team at Worzalla Printing. They brought skill and professionalism to this enterprise. And the final product is something that we are all very proud of.

I am also deeply indebted to everyone who provided reviews and testimonials for this project. In particular I want to thank the wonderful Tanya Queiro, who was the first to agree to do so. I am honored and humbled by their participation and very kind words.

The men and women who serve this country in uniform deserve every ounce of gratitude and every accolade that this great and grateful nation can muster. Their loved ones deserve even more than that. We should embrace them all so that they always know that their enormous sacrifice is appreciated.

Finally, I want to thank my wife, Diane, for her support and involvement in this project. The decision to make this part of our personal life public was not an easy one. But, once the decision was made, her participation was invaluable. You might say that this book serves as a gigantic thank you note to her for helping me through that ordeal 20 years ago. So, I won't belabor the point. I will simply say that I am glad that she was married to me then, and I am glad that she is married to me now.

APPENDIX A

"Perspectives From a Soldier in the Gulf"
Published in the Shawano Evening Leader, The Columbus Ledger-Enquirer,
and the Savannah Morning News, *Nov. 1990*

I am an American soldier currently deployed in the Saudi Arabian desert. More specifically I am serving as the adjutant of an armor battalion in the 197th Infantry Brigade out in the middle of nowhere. And I mean nowhere...

I'm sure by now the chronicles of our mission here have receded from the front page headlines. With my limited understanding of the journalism business, I acknowledge the fact that there is a big wide world of news going on out there that was bound to supplant stories about the crisis in the gulf sooner or later. This perspective is just a subtle reminder to those other than our families that we're still here completely uncertain of what lies ahead. And while some of the service members living here live in barracks with running water and toilet facilities, the vast majority of us are doing without.

This is not a plea for sympathy or anything of the kind. I am a soldier. Subsequently, I have come to expect living under less than ideal conditions. As far as I'm concerned it comes with the territory. After all, I volunteered for this. If we are able to return home without firing a shot this deployment will serve to solidify the fact that this is our job. This is what we are paid to do. And if we didn't know if before, I believe that all of us now have an acute understanding that freedom is not free. There are sacrifices that must be made. There is a price that has to be paid.

Eighteen months ago I had the privilege of being in Normandy, France, for the 45th anniversary of the allied invasion that spearheaded the liberation of Europe. As I walked through the cemetery on Omaha Beach where nearly 10,000 fellow Americans are buried.

I was sobered by the gravity of the word sacrifice. These men had made the ultimate sacrifice so that freedom and liberty might endure. Likewise, I was sobered by the fact that I, as a soldier, might be called upon to make the same sacrifice.

And so here I sit, with thousands of my brothers and sisters in arms in complete uncertainty. I don't know if I'll ever see my wife and family again. I'd like to believe that I will. But, at this point I don't know. Gen. William Tecumseh Sherman once said that "war is hell." Waiting for war I'm sure pales by comparison. But, I can assure you that it's no picnic. At this point only God knows how events will unfold.

As a student of history I have marveled at the resolve displayed by our fore bearers during World War II. For four years our fellow Americans bore the burden and ultimately became victorious. I was born in 1963, long after the Korean War had ended. And I have virtually no personal recollection of the Vietnam War. But I do know that the outcome of those wars and the events that surrounded them (especially Vietnam) were less than ideal.

And those outcomes have served to forestall nearly every military operation since then.

Since I accepted my commission in June 1983 I've been conducting my own highly unscientific study of the American people, trying to determine if the resolve displayed by our fore bearers in World War II would reappear if we ever had to face the prospect of another protracted conflict. Until August of this year I had come to the conclusion that the resolve would not return. I believed that we as a people had in essence become fat, dumb and happy. We had become soft and spoiled. We had become a people with seemingly no interest or concern about events that occurred outside our personal worlds.

Mine was a very dim outlook. As a soldier I felt that the American people had no concept of what I did or the sacrifices made by me and those like me day in and day out, year after year.

But, now I am happy to report emphatically that I was wrong. Since this crisis began all of my doubts and misgivings have been dispelled. I have been personally moved by the outpouring of support and the kindness that has been displayed toward us all. As my unit left Ft. Benning I was touched by the throngs of people that lined the overpasses along I-185 to show their support. Likewise, I've been touched by the volume of cards and letters, candy and baked goods that we have received from all over the country as evidence of that support.

And so we continue to sit here in the desert, thousands of miles from all the things we know and love, still not knowing what the future will bring. But, as the desert winter approaches we can be warmed by the knowledge that we have the full support and confidence of the people of our country. This is a knowledge that our Vietnam era brethren did not know, and for that I feel personally and truly sorry. It means everything.

As a leader my biggest concern now is for the morale of the soldiers as this odyssey continues. But, I know that our trust in God and our country will help carry us triumphantly through whatever lies ahead.

I have a wife who I love and miss very much. I have family a friends all over the country who are concerned for my well being. I have two brothers who are also soldiers who are not here presently, but may very well join me in the desert if events dictate. I harbor dreams and aspirations that lie far beyond the realm of visions of battlefield glory.

I have a very keen interest in government and governing. And I pray for our president as he grapples with the monumental choices and decisions that must be made. At this juncture I do not envy his position. But, he has my complete faith and confidence.

Singer Lee Greenwood's powerful rendition of the song "God Bless the USA" captures the essence of how many of us feel: *And I'm proud to be an American, where at least I know I'm free. And I won't forget the men who died, who gave that right to me. And I'll gladly stand up next to you and defend her still today. 'Cause there ain't no doubt I love this land, God bless the USA.*

Please continue to pray for our safe return.

DEAR DIANE

APPENDIX B

"Reflections on the Vietnam War Memorial"
Published in the **Shawano Leader,** *Dec. 30, 1991*

I did not serve in Vietnam. Nor do I personally know anyone that died in that conflict. However, my generation of soldiers did have "our war:" the recent conflict in The Persian Gulf. Last year at this time I was on the sands of the Arabian Peninsula contemplating an uncertain future.

Fortunately for this country and for those of us who served there, our campaign had the overwhelming support of the American people. The war was quickly decisive and was executed successfully with a minimum loss of life on the allied side. For that we should be grateful. Unfortunately, this was not the case with the war in Vietnam.

Recently, I was in Washington, D.C., for the first time and visited the Vietnam Memorial. It was the day after Veterans Day and as I slowly walked past that monument to those who had fallen I could not help but be moved. Despite the fact that there was not a single name on that wall that impacted upon my life in any way, I found myself fighting hard to hold back the tears. Why? Because there were in fact over 58,000 souls whose names appeared on that wall that I, in only the most remote and distant way, shared a kinship with. That being the spirit of the noble warrior.

I use the phrase remote and distant kinship because I know that the survivors of that conflict share a bond that is much stronger and more immediate to their fallen comrades than I ever will. And I would never presume to encroach upon that.

Yet, I know that a kinship between this era and that one does exist.

It transcends time and place and even generation. I know because it was looking me in the face on that day just a few weeks ago.

Much time, energy and emotion has been expended trying to determine the causes and effects of the Vietnam War. My professional military education has exposed me to certain aspects of the war. My personal reading has exposed me to others.

After reading works such as *No More Vietnams* by Richard Nixon, *A Bright and Shining Lie* by Neil Sheehan, *Counsel to the President* by Clark Clifford, *About Face* by Col. David Hackworth, *Reunion* by Tom Hayden, and other works, I feel I've considered enough different viewpoints to form my own opinions about the causes and effects of the Vietnam War. However, I will not state them. They are not relevant. That is not my focus here.

Rather, it is to focus on the men and women who served, fought, sustained the wounds, and died there in a land so far away from home. They were there for different reasons but the reasons do not matter. What matters is that they were there, willing to pay the blood price, willing to make the ultimate sacrifice.

It has been stated that Operation Desert Storm served more than just the purpose of expelling the Iraqi Army from Kuwait. Some say that it also served as a final catharsis for a nation still trying to come to terms with a pain over Vietnam that had not completely subsided. I don't know if that is true. Certainly, there are people more qualified than me to make that judgement.

However, I do know this. On March 29, 1991, when the plane bringing me and my comrades home from the Kingdom of Saudi Arabia landed in Bangor, Maine, it seemed as if the whole town had come out to greet us. Among the crowd of well wishers were some Vietnam veterans. Some were in wheelchairs. Some were missing appendages, no doubt sacrificed on the field of battle. Some were attired in the uniforms of their era.

Others were in civilian clothes adorned with campaign medals. And as we fellowshipped with the crowd, those veterans reached out to embrace us and said, "Welcome home, brother. WELCOME HOME."

It was one of the most moving experiences of my life. And I knew then that a bond indeed existed.

On November 12, 1991, I was considering these things as I walked along the Vietnam Memorial. And on that day, at that particular point in time, I did the only thing that I was capable of doing. I cried.

APPENDIX C

"Farewell Address to the 1st Battalion 69th Armor"
Delivered Sept. 30, 1989, Kitzingen, West Germany

The following speech was delivered as part of a military tradition called "Hail and Farewell." The "hail" part comes as new officers were entering the battalion, with the "farewell" marking an officer's departure from a battalion. This is my farewell speech.

LTC Coon, thanks for the kind words.

Three years is a long time. Goodbye is very difficult.

I came here three years ago already a first lieutenant by virtue of my experience in the National Guard. But I can say that it has been here in this battalion that I feel I have matured both as an officer and a man. And it is an experience that I am eternally grateful for.

Now, I suppose I could stand here at this time and say that every day has been a good day. That all the times have been good times. And that all the people have been good people. But, that is simply not true. And I believe that a time like this requires complete candor.

Every day has not been a good day. All the times have not been good times. And all the people have not been good people. There have been days when I have asked myself, what's the point? But, that's life.

However, I can say this, in complete candor. That is that the good days have far exceeded the bad days. The good times have far exceeded the bad times. And far and away, without a doubt, the good people have been truly incredible.

Therein lies the strength of this battalion. It is not the tanks in the motor pool, the Bradleys, or the mortar tracks. It is the people. And I believe that if a man can find this type of work environment anywhere, he can consider himself very lucky. And that is exactly how I feel right now.

Two final thoughts if I may.

First, in the time that we have been here Diane and I have managed to make some good friends. And I feel like they know who they are. Therefore, I do not feel encumbered by the need to mention any names. To them I say as I look toward the future the prospect of continuing those friendships as we get older and hopefully wiser fills me with a great deal of anticipation. This departure is by no means an ending. And I assure you that the best is yet to come.

Finally, to those of you whom I never have the chance to see again or work with again, let me say that it is been my distinct privilege and honor to walk among you and work among you these past three years. And I will seize upon this opportunity to wish all of you God's speed, and the very best of everything.

God bless the speed and power battalion. And God bless the United States of America.

Thank you.